The Charms of TEA

REMINISCENCES & RECIPES

The Charms *of* TEA

REMINISCENCES & RECIPES

From the Editors
of Victoria
Magazine

HEARST BOOKS

A Division of Sterling Publishing Co., Inc.

NEW YORK

Produced by Smallwood & Stewart, Inc., New York City
Editor: Alice Wong
Designer: Barbara Scott-Goodman
Contributors: Mary Goodbody, Linda Sunshine, and Catherine Revland

Library of Congress Cataloging-in-Publication Data
Available upon request.

10 9 8 7 6 5 4 3 2 1

First Paperback Edition 2003
Published by Hearst Books
A Division of Sterling Publishing Co., Inc.
387 Park Avenue South, New York, NY 10016

Victoria is a trademark owned by Hearst Magazines Property, Inc., in USA,
and Hearst Communications, Inc., in Canada. Hearst Books is a trademark
owned by Hearst Communications, Inc.

Distributed in Canada by Sterling Publishing
c/o Canadian Manda Group, One Atlantic Avenue, Suite 105
Toronto, Ontario, Canada M6K 3E7

Distributed in Australia by Capricorn Link (Australia) Pty. Ltd.
P.O. Box 704, Windsor, NSW 2756 Australia

Manufactured in Singapore

ISBN 1-58816-311-3

CONTENTS

FOREWORD

Whenever the fragrance rises from a fresh-poured cup of tea, a sense of comfort, peace, and ceremony accompanies it. Perhaps that's why, in most of the world, the taking and offering of tea signifies trust and friendship. It's an occasion, a moment of calm to which the harsher realities are simply not invited. In fact, ever since this beguiling beverage from China was introduced to Holland and England, teatime has been a social and civilizing event, giving rise to implements so elegantly wrought that we prize them—and use them—to this day.

Adapting the traditions of tea to our own lives is what keeps a good thing going. Some pretty cups, your grandmother's sugar tongs? These and a slice of pound cake can make a party out of a chat with a friend at the kitchen table. Or consider giving a baby-shower tea (with plenty of cucumber sandwiches) or hosting an after-sledding gathering by the fire with hot spiced tea and gingerbread.

We at *Victoria* Magazine have always celebrated the many joys of tea. This book is a chance to share these timeless pleasures with you. You'll find gloriously photographed ideas for enjoying a proper English cream tea, as well as pages of recipes for scrumptious sweets and savories you can make. And it's all served up with delightful excerpts from renowned authors who appreciate just what you do—friendship, beauty, and a really good cup of tea.

The Editors of *Victoria*

INTRODUCTION

As the light wanes between the hours of four and six in the afternoon, the sounds of a whistling kettle, the clink of sugar dropped from a tong into a thin porcelain cup, the fragrance of freshly brewing jasmine or aromatic Darjeeling tea, and the words "Cream or lemon?" are enough to instantly soothe the spirits of the many people who have made a ritual of partaking in the charms of the Victorian tea.

The custom of the afternoon tea has been popular among civilized people for centuries, but Victorian eating habits, of a hearty breakfast, light lunch and late dinner, made it a necessity of life. Over the years, the English developed that necessity to perfection, promoted and sanctioned by Queen Victoria herself.

To be truly Victorian, the tea must be properly brewed, the food sumptuous, and the setting elegant. The food served at the traditional Victorian tea is ultra-indulgent: The pastry crust is sweet, to say nothing of the butter-rich scones, shortbreads, and crumpets dripping with honey. On the other hand, the portions are small. The many kinds of dainty morsels on the tray are meant to chasten the appetite, not conquer it, and the rich fare can be substituted with the equally traditional slice of cucumber or sprig of watercress served on a bit of bread with herbed butter.

When the American Victorians adopted the ritual of afternoon tea, they retained its regal elegance. Once a day, out came all the finest pieces of china in the closet: the treasured coin silver sugar tongs, the cut glass cream-and-sugar from a favorite aunt, or the Billingsley rose china displayed on the best linens and hand-crocheted laces. One of the great joys of the Victorian tea is giving regular use to the precious heirlooms that can languish on shelves for years, putting a family in daily touch with its own traditions and the legacies of loved ones from the past.

In *The Charms of Tea,* the editors of *Victoria* magazine invite you to rediscover the joys of this enduring tradition, through sumptuous art and photographs, plus much of the literature which celebrates it. We have turned to such beloved writers as Daphne du Maurier, J. M. Barrie, Charles Lamb, Henry James, and Marcel Proust, who immortalized the madeleine dipped in a poignant memory of a childhood afternoon tea. As well we include authentic recipes and precise directions for brewing the perfect cup.

From a spot of tea in solitude to the formal high tea, a resplendent affair, the Victorian afternoon tea reflects that serene and gracious era. It is above all a comforting ritual, simultaneously soothing and stimulating, in which to withdraw momentarily from the busyness of our lives and pay gentle homage to the passage of time.

THE VICTORIAN TEA

In nothing more is the English genius for domesticity more notably declared than in the institution of this festival—almost one may call it—of afternoon tea ... The mere chink of cups and saucers tunes the mind to happy repose.

George Gissing
THE PRIVATE PAPERS OF HENRY RYECROFT

THE VICTORIAN TEA

The Englishness of the Victorian tea is baked right into the sweets and savories that are traditionally served, for many have place names like Dundee and Eccles cakes, Cornish pasties, Shrewsberry cookies, or Coventry tarts. Other recipes can be traced back to the court of Henry the Eighth. The custom of "taking" tea was championed by the English in the time of the "merry monarch," Charles II, whose wife, the Portuguese Princess Catherine of Braganza, came to London with a large chest of tea as part of her dowry. But tea was precious in the seventeenth century, and remained too expensive an item to be consumed by anyone but the aristocracy until it began to be brought by clipper ships, those exotic and romantic three-masted vessels that raced across the oceans of the world during the height of the British empire. By the nineteenth century, many a British subject was enjoying this once exotic beverage, and the delights of bold, brisk Assam, delicate Darjeeling, golden Ceylon, or aromatic jasmine, whose flowers open and bloom in the teapot, had become part of everyday life.

But it was Queen Victoria who popularized the custom of taking afternoon tea. During Victoria's long reign, no loyal subject of the British Empire neglected to take a substantial afternoon tea, as unlikely an event as neglecting to take their umbrellas on a misty day. Sponge cake was the Queen's favorite sweet, served with a layer of strawberry jam and whipped cream, and she also popularized the custom of drinking tea with a slice of lemon, which she brought home from the Russian court where she had been visiting her eldest daughter, the Princess Royal.

Soon the call of "You must come to tea" was echoing in every rank of society, and Victorians throughout the realm knew that to steep the beverage properly you "bring the teapot to the kettle, not the kettle to the pot." In even the humblest working class cottage the custom was observed with as much elegance and charm as could be afforded. With the invention of spode, everyone could possess a beautiful translucent tea set, with cups thin enough to see the shadow of one's fingers through them, and many a hand-painted tea pot bore the inscription "God Bless Our Queen."

In the more than sixty years of Queen Victoria's reign, the afternoon tea had become a national pastime. When the clock struck four, every kettle in the empire began to whistle and every tea table was set with all manner of delectables to appease the appetite and restore the flagging spirit, an egalitarian legacy few monarchs could surpass. The observance had become a treasured custom, a moment best described by Charles Dickens as one "in which we were perfectly contented with ourselves and one another."

*A hardened and
shameless tea-drinker, who has for twenty years diluted
his meals with only the infusion of this fascinating
plant; whose kettle has scarcely time to cool; who with
tea amuses the evening, with tea solaces the midnight,
and with tea welcomes the morning.*

Samuel Johnson

There was an old quiet smell about the room, as though the air in it was little changed, for all the sweet lilac scent and the roses brought to it throughout the early summer. Whatever air came to this room, whether from the garden or from the sea, would lose its first freshness, becoming part of the unchanging room itself, one with the books, musty and never read, one with the scrolled ceiling, the dark panelling, the heavy curtains.

It was an ancient mossy smell, the smell of a silent church where services are seldom held, where rusty lichen grows upon the stones and ivy tendrils creep to the very windows. A room for peace, a room for meditation.

Soon tea was brought to us, a stately little performance enacted by Frith and the young footman, in which I played no part until they had gone, and while Maxim glanced through his great pile of letters I played with two dripping crumpets, crumbled cake with my hands, and swallowed my scalding tea . . .

We should grow old here together, we should sit like this to our tea as old people, Maxim and I, with other dogs, the successors of these, and the library would wear the same ancient musty smell that it did now. It would know a period of glorious shabbiness and wear when the boys were young — our boys — for I saw them sprawling on the sofa with muddy boots, bringing with them always a litter of rods, and cricket bats, great clasp-knives, bows-and-arrows . . .

My vision was disturbed by the opening of the door, and Frith came in with the footman to clear the tea.

Daphne du Maurier
REBECCA

There came a knock at the door, and the butler entered with a laden tea tray and set it down upon a small Japanese table. There was a rattle of cups and saucers and the hissing of a fluted Georgian urn. Two globe-shaped china dishes were brought in by a page. Dorian Gray went over and poured out the tea. The two men sauntered languidly to the table, and examined what was under the covers.

"Let us go to the theater tonight," said Lord Henry. "There is sure to be something on, somewhere. I have promised to dine at White's, but it is only with an old friend, so I can send him a wire to say that I am ill, or that I am prevented from coming in consequence of a subsequent engagement. I think that would be a rather nice excuse: it would have all the surprise of candour."

"It is such a bore putting on one's dress-clothes," muttered Hallward. "And, when one has them on, they are so horrid."

"Yes," answered Lord Henry, dreamily, "the costume of the nineteenth century is detestable. It is so sombre, so depressing. Sin is the only real colour element left in modern life."

"You really must not say things like that before Dorian, Harry."

"Before which Dorian? The one who is pouring out tea for us, or the other one in the picture?"

Oscar Wilde
THE PICTURE OF DORIAN GRAY

*C*ome, little cottage girl, you seem
To want a cup of tea;
And will you take a little cream?
Now tell the truth to me."

She had a rustic, woodland grin
Her cheek was soft as silk,
And she replied, "Sir, please, put in
A little drop of milk."

Barry Pain
WORDSWORTH

*L*ove and scandal are the best sweeteners of tea.

Henry Fielding
LOVE IN SEVERAL MASQUES

*T*hank God for tea!

What would the world do without tea? — how did it exist?

I am glad I was not born before tea.

Rev. Sydney Smith
LADY HOLLAND'S MEMOIR

I believe it is customary in good society to take some
slight refreshment at five o'clock.

Oscar Wilde
THE IMPORTANCE OF BEING EARNEST

Under certain circumstances there are few hours in life more agreeable than the hour dedicated to the ceremony known as afternoon tea. There are circumstances in which, whether you partake of the tea or not — some people of course never do, — the situation is in itself delightful. Those that I have in mind . . . offered an admirable setting to an innocent pastime. The implements of the little feast had been disposed upon the lawn of an old English country-house, in what I should call the perfect middle of a splendid summer afternoon. Part of the afternoon had waned, but much of it was left, and what was left was of the finest and rarest quality. Real dusk would not arrive for many hours; but the flood of summer light had begun to ebb, the air had grown mellow, the shadows were long upon the smooth, dense turf. They lengthened slowly, however, and the scene expressed that sense of leisure still to come which is perhaps the chief source of one's enjoyment of such a scene at such an hour. From five o'clock to eight is on certain occasions a little eternity; but on such an occasion as this the interval could be only an eternity of pleasure. The persons concerned in it were taking their pleasure quietly, and they were not of the sex which is supposed to furnish the regular votaries of the ceremony I have mentioned. The shadows on the perfect lawn were straight and angular: they were the shadows of an old man sitting in a deep wicker-chair near the low table on which the tea had been served, and of two younger men strolling to and fro, in desultory talk, in front of him. The old man had his cup in his hand; it was an unusually large cup, of a different pattern from the rest of the set and painted in brilliant colours. He disposed of its contents with much circumspection, holding it for a long time close to his chin, with his face turned to the house. His companions had either finished their tea or were indifferent to their privilege; they smoked cigarettes as they continued to stroll.

Henry James
THE PORTRAIT OF A LADY

THE SOCIAL TEA

A t last the secret is out,
as it always must come in the end,
The delicious story is ripe to tell an intimate friend;
Over tea-cups and in the square the tongue has its desire;
Still waters run deep, my dear,
there's never smoke without fire.

W.H. Auden
THE TWELVE SONGS
VIII

THE SOCIAL TEA

In the Victorian Age late afternoon was the time people visited each other in their homes, with motivations that ranged from the fulfilling of social obligations to impassioned courting. In order to avoid confusion, the custom was to choose a day to be officially "at home." They also followed that most Victorian of traditions, leaving behind beautifully designed and embossed calling cards on silver trays in the front halls of those who were out calling themselves. There was a certain amount of satisfaction in coming home to a tray filled with the cards of those who had come calling.

As a social event, the Victorian tea was customarily limited to matters that were light-hearted in nature. This was not the time for heated political discussion or the airing of family feuds, and while gossip was inevitable, it was never harsh or mean in spirit. In every way, the demeanor of the hour reflected the regal elegance that had always been the essence of taking tea. Bread was cut as thin as the porcelain cups which held the fragrant beverages, and at its most luxurious, the food and drink was served by footmen as musicians played in the background. Women wore soft, diaphanous tea gowns, lacy and loose-waisted. In every way, taking tea was a time to momentarily set aside the mundane and the ordinary and give grace and charm to the course of an afternoon.

The intimacy of the setting made it natural for falling in love. Tea-for-two remains a favorite form of early courtship, and many a romance has blossomed over two cups of steaming tea and a plate of meringue kisses. Afternoon tea is also a natural time for getting together with close friends, when reading tea leaves is mandatory and secrets can be safely exchanged. The tea can also expand to make a grand social statement, culminating in the weekend high tea. This occasion is as close to dinner as teatime comes, all the while remaining more truly elegant in setting. High tea is traditionally served at six o'clock, and it is the perfect way to invite people for an hour or two before an evening's entertainment.

From bridal showers to baby christenings to birthday parties to open house for out of town guests, afternoon tea is an occasion for everyone, especially the children. In Victorian times, custom dictated that children took tea with their nanny in the nursery, shut off from the parents. Happily, children and parents now share this special time together. Little ones do love to emulate adult behavior, carefully wrapping chubby fingers around their cups of weak tea well laced with milk or honey.

From a cozy tea-for-two to a gathering of many, the Victorian afternoon tea envelops all with an aura of warmth and comfort. The pouring of steaming beverages, the passing of sweets and savories, and the sharing of intimacies and light-hearted conversation make this very special time of the day one of life's finest pleasures.

One day in winter, as I came home, my mother, seeing that I was cold, offered me some tea, a thing I did not ordinarily take. I declined at first, and then, for no particular reason, changed my mind. She sent out for one of those short, plump little cakes called 'petites madeleines,' which look as though they had been moulded in the fluted scallop of a pilgrim's shell. And soon, mechanically, weary after a dull day with the prospect of a depressing morrow, I raised to my lips a spoonful of the tea in which I had soaked a morsel of the cake. No sooner had the warm liquid, and the crumbs with it, touched on my palate than a shudder ran through my whole body, and I stopped, intent upon the extraordinary changes that were taking place. An exquisite pleasure had invaded my senses . . . I had ceased now to feel mediocre, accidental, mortal. Whence could it have come to me, this all-powerful joy? I was conscious that it was connected with the taste of tea and cake, but that it infinitely transcended those savours, could not, indeed, be of the same nature as theirs. Whence did it come? What did it signify? How could I seize upon and define it?

I drink a second mouthful, in which I find nothing more than in the first, a third, which gives me rather less than the second. It is time to stop; the potion is losing its magic. It is plain that the object of my quest, the truth, lies not in the cup but in myself.

Marcel Proust
SWANN'S WAY

I could have introduced you to some very beautiful people. Mrs. Langtry and Lady Lonsdale and a lot of clever beings who were at tea with me.

Oscar Wilde

The Baroness found it amusing to go to tea; she dressed as if for dinner. The tea-table offered an anomalous and picturesque repast; and on leaving it they all sat and talked in the large piazza, or wandered about the garden in the star-light, with their ears full of those sounds of strange insects which, though they are supposed to be, all over the world, a part of the magic of summer nights, seemed to the Baroness to have, beneath these western skies, an incomparable resonance.

Henry James
THE EUROPEANS

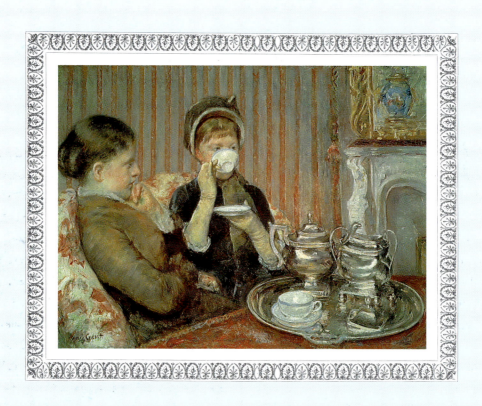

Half-past four. A frown of dissatisfaction settled on James Cushat-Prinkly's face. He would arrive at the Sebastable mansion just at the hour of afternoon tea. Joan would be seated at a low table, spread with an array of silver kettles and cream-jugs and delicate porcelain teacups, behind which her voice would tinkle pleasantly in a series of little friendly questions about weak or strong tea, how much, if any, sugar, milk, cream and so forth. "Is it one lump? I forgot. You do take milk, don't you? Would you like some more hot water, if it's too strong?"

Cushat-Prinkly had read of such things in scores of novels, and hundreds of actual experiences had told him that they were true to life. Thousands of women, at this solemn afternoon hour, were sitting behind dainty porcelain and silver fittings, with their voices tinkling pleasantly in a cascade of solic-itous little questions. Cushat-Prinkly detested the whole system of afternoon tea. According to his theory of life a woman should lie on a divan or couch, talking with incomparable charm, or looking unutterable thoughts, or merely silent as a thing to be looked on, and from behind a silken curtain a small Nubian page should silently bring in a tray with cups and dainties, to be accepted silently, as a matter of course, without drawn-out chatter about cream and sugar and hot water. If one's soul was really enslaved at one's mistress's feet, how could one talk coherently about weakened tea? Cushat-Prinkly had never expounded his views on the subject to his mother, all her life she had been accustomed to tinkle pleasantly at tea-time behind dainty porcelain and silver, and if he had spoke to her about divans and Nubian pages she would have urged him to take a week's holiday at the seaside.

Saki (H. H. Munro)
TEA

This meal happened to be a make-believe tea, and they sat round the board, guzzling in their greed; and really, what with their chatter and recriminations, the noise, as Wendy said, was positively deafening. To be sure, she did not mind noise, but she simply would not have them grabbing things, and then excusing themselves by saying that Tootles had pushed their elbow. There was a fixed rule that they must never hit back at meals, but should refer the matter of dispute to Wendy by raising the right arm politely and saying, "I complain of So-and-so"; but what usually happened was that they forgot to do this or did it too much.

"Silence," cried Wendy when for the twentieth time she had told them that they were not all to speak at once. "Is your calabash empty, Slightly, darling?"

"Not quite empty, Mummy," Slightly said, after looking into an imaginary mug.

"He hasn't even begun to drink his milk," Nibs interposed.

This was telling, and Slightly seized his chance.

"I complain of Nibs," he cried promptly.

John, however, had held up his hand first.

"Well, John?"

"May I sit in Peter's chair, as he is not here?"

"Sit in father's chair, John!" Wendy was scandalized. "Certainly not."

"He is not really our father," John answered. "He didn't even know how a father does till I showed him."

This was grumbling. "We complain of John," cried the twins.

Tootles held up his hand. He was so much the humblest of them, indeed he was the only humble one, that Wendy was specially gentle with him.

"I don't suppose," Tootles said diffidently,

"that I could be father."

"No, Tootles."

Once Tootles began, which was not very often, he had a silly way of going on.

"As I can't be father," he said heavily, "I don't suppose, Michael, you would let me be baby?"

"No, I won't," Michael rapped out. He was already in his basket.

"As I can't be baby," Tootles said, getting heavier and heavier, "do you think I could be a twin?"

"No, indeed," replied the twins; "it's awfully difficult to be a twin."

"As I can't be anything important," said Tootles, "would any of you like to see me do a trick?"

"No," they all replied.

Then at last he stopped. "I hadn't really any hope," he said.

The hateful telling broke out again.

"Slightly is coughing on the table."

"The twins began with mammee-apples."

"Curly is taking both tappa rolls and yams."

"Nibs is speaking with his mouth full."

"I complain of the twins."

"I complain of Curly."

"I complain of Nibs."

"Oh dear, oh dear," cried Wendy, "I'm sure I sometimes think that children are more trouble than they are worth."

She told them to clear away, and sat down to her workbasket: a heavy load of stockings and every knee with a hole in it as usual.

J.M. Barrie
PETER PAN

The maid led him through the darkness of the drawing room to the terrace in the patio, where he saw Fermina Daza sitting beside a small table set for two. She offered him tea, chocolate, or coffee. Florentino Ariza asked for coffee, very hot and very strong, and she told the maid: "The usual for me." The usual was a strong infusion of different kinds of Oriental teas, which raised her spirits after her siesta. By the time she had emptied the teapot and the coffeepot, they had both attempted and then broken off several topics of conversation, not so much because they were really interested in them but in order to avoid others that neither dared to broach. They were both intimidated, they could not understand what they were doing so far from their youth . . . It was the first time in half a century that they had been so close and had enough time to look at each other with some serenity, and they had seen each other for what they were: two old people, ambushed by death, who had nothing in common except the memory of an ephemeral past that was no longer theirs . . . and so he returned on Tuesday at five o'clock, and then every Tuesday after that, and he ignored the convention of notifying her, because by the end of the second month the weekly visits had been incorporated into both their routines. Florentino Ariza brought English biscuits for tea, candied chestnuts, Greek olives, little salon delicacies that he would find on the ocean liners. One Tuesday he brought her a copy of the picture of her and Hildebranda taken by the Belgian photographer more than half a century before, which he had bought for fifteen centavos at a postcard sale in the Arcade of the Scribes. Fermina Daza could not understand how it had come to be there, and he could only understand it as a miracle of love.

Gabriel García Márquez
LOVE IN THE TIME OF CHOLERA

THE PROPER SETTING

The cozy fire is bright and gay,
The merry kettle boils away
    And hums a cheerful song.
I sing the saucer and the cup;
Pray, Mary, fill the teapot up,
    And do not make it strong.

Barry Pain
THE POETS AT TEA

THE PROPER SETTING

Ladies of the Victorian and Edwardian eras served tea from ornate silver services in the drawing room, customarily in front of the hearth. The lady of the house did the pouring, and the setting was formal indeed. Today, as long as the setting is gracious and elegant, the tea party can take place anywhere you wish.

If there are to be many guests and a grand assortment of foods, forsake the delicate tea table for the dining room and let your guests serve themselves. They can then settle themselves in one of the groupings of chairs arranged in the living room to encourage cozy chatter. Lay one or two sparkling white linen or lace tablecloths over the table, set sandwiches and cookies out on your prettiest plates, bundle hot muffins and scones in baskets lined with crisp linens, and arrange masterpieces like elaborately decorated cakes on pedestal stands, so they may be fully admired. Arrange teacups near the teapot with spoons nestled in their saucers, and stack dessert-sized plates and forks for guests to fill with delicious treats. Do not worry if all the china does not match. Two and even three complementary patterns are acceptable, particularly if they are of the finest quality. Mugs, however, will not do. Tea tastes best when sipped from thin bone china. Do not forget soft and snowy linen napkins. One of the joys of collecting antique linen lies in the fact that its patina cannot be replicated, but softens slowly, with age and many washings.

In the summer, the glories of tea *al fresco* should be thoroughly explored. The front porch, the back terrace, the gazebo, or an arrangement of garden chairs around a table set under a shady tree are all most conducive to a summertime tea.

Crisp bright autumn afternoons are a wonderful time for a picnic tea. Pack a hamper with tea sandwiches and portable sweets, a light checkered tablecloth and a large blanket, fill one thermos with hot tea and another with cold milk, add a few packets of sugar and a lemon to slice on a spot, and you're off to enjoy one of the most pleasant aspects of the afternoon tea, its great portability.

If you are planning a classic English tea, you too may decide on serving it in your living room, particularly if the weather is cold and you have a hearth. Wintertime seems to demand that tea be drunk close to a merry fire. Intimate teas between dear friends can be served in the bedroom, especially if it has a fireplace. That was the setting of the original teas held by the Duchess of Bedford in the late 1700s. Faint with hunger, she and her friends withdrew to her private rooms to partake furtively of rich foods in order to sustain themselves until dinnertime. The need to be furtive has gone, but the formal bedroom-with-fireplace setting remains a most inviting setting for tea. What is the proper setting for a Victorian tea? The answer is simple: one that is chosen for its graciousness and lovingly prepared.

In a few minutes tea was brought. Very delicate was the china, very old the plate, very thin the bread-and-butter, and very small the lumps of sugar. Sugar was evidently Mrs. Jamieson's favourite economy. I question if the little filigree sugar-tongs, made something like scissors, could have opened themselves wide enough to take up an honest, vulgar, good-size piece; and when I tried to seize two little minnikin pieces at once, so as not to be detected in too many returns to the sugar-basin, they absolutely dropped one, with a little sharp clatter, quite in a malicious and unnatural manner. But before this happened, we had had a slight disappointment. In the little silver jug was cream, in the larger one was milk. As soon as Mr. Mulliner came in,

Carlo began to beg, which was a thing our manners forbade us to do, though I am sure we were just as hungry; and Mrs. Jamieson said she was certain we would excuse her if she gave her poor dumb Carlo his tea first. She accordingly mixed a saucerful for him, and put it down for him to lap; and then she told us how intelligent and sensible the dear little fellow was; he knew cream quite well, and constantly refused tea with only milk in it. So the milk was left for us; but we silently thought we were quite as intelligent and sensible as Carlo, and felt as if insult were added to injury when we were called upon to admire the gratitude evinced by his wagging his tail for the cream which should have been ours.

Mrs. Gaskell
CRANFORD

The pouring is usually done by close friends of the hostess. These ladies are asked beforehand if they will "do the honors," and unless they have a very valid reason, they should accept. Sometimes, after an hour, the first two are relieved by two other friends of the hostess.

It does not matter that a guest going into the dining room does not know the deputy hostesses who are pouring. Each person walks right up to the table and says, "May I have a cup of tea?"

The one pouring should smile and answer, "Certainly! How do you like it? Strong or weak? Would you like cream or lemon?"

If the visitor says, "Weak," boiling water is added, and according to the guest's wishes, sugar, cream or lemon.

Elizabeth L. Post
THE NEW EMILY POST'S ETIQUETTE

A weekly "At Home" tea is served upon small tables, the servant, before bringing it in, seeing that one is placed conveniently near his mistress, who generally dispenses the tea. No plates are given for a tea of this kind, and the servant, after seeing that all is in readiness, leaves the room, the gentleman of the party doing all the waiting that is necessary.

The tea equipage is usually placed upon a silver-salver, the hot water is in a small silver or china kettle on a stand, and the cups are small. Thin bread and butter, cake, petits-fours and sometimes fresh fruit are all the eatables given. These are daintily arranged on plates, spread with lace doilies, and placed in a cakestand or on a convenient table.

Mrs. Beeton
THE BOOK OF HOUSEHOLD MANAGEMENT

BONNARD, Pierre. *The Breakfast Room.* (c. 1930–31) Oil on canvas, 62⅞ × 44⅞″ (159.6 × 113.8 cm). Collection, The Museum of Modern Art, New York. Given anonymously.

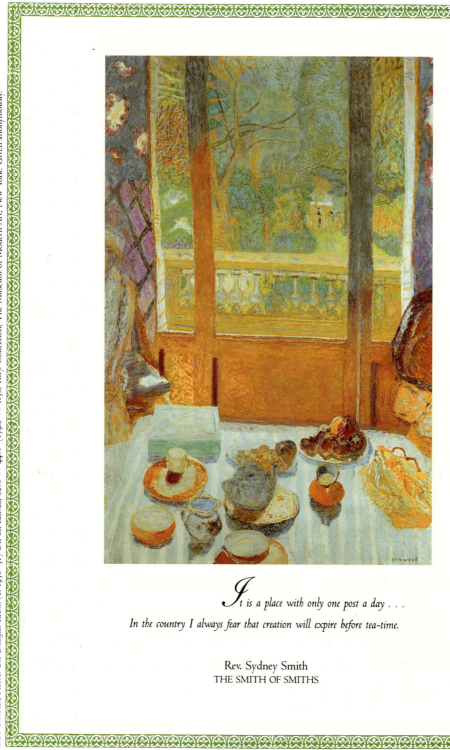

*I*t is a place with only one post a day . . .

In the country I always fear that creation will expire before tea-time.

Rev. Sydney Smith
THE SMITH OF SMITHS

You can ask Diana to come over and spend the afternoon with you and have tea here."

"Oh, Marilla!" Anne clasped her hands. "How perfectly lovely! You *are* able to imagine things after all or else you'd never have understood how I've longed for that very thing. It will seem so nice and grown-uppish. No fear of my forgetting to put the tea to draw when I have company. Oh, Marilla, can I use the rosebud spray tea set?"

"No, indeed! The rosebud tea set! Well, what next? You know I never use that except for the minister or the Aids. You'll put down the old brown tea set. But you can open the little yellow crock of cherry preserves. It's time it was being used anyhow — I believe it's beginning to work. And you can cut some fruit-cake and have some of the cookies and snaps."

"I can just imagine myself sitting down at the head of the table and pouring out the tea," said Anne, shutting her eyes ecstatically. "And asking Diana if she takes sugar! I know she doesn't but of course I'll ask her just as if I didn't know. And then pressing her to take another piece of fruitcake and another helping of preserves. Oh, Marilla, it's a wonderful sensation just to think of it. Can I take her into the spare room to lay off her hat when she comes? And then into the parlor to sit?"

"No. The sitting-room will do for you and your company. But there's a bottle half full of raspberry cordial that was left over from the church social the other night. It's on the second shelf of the sitting room closet and you and Diana can have it if you like, and a cooky to eat with it along in the afternoon . . ."

Anne flew down to the hollow, past the Dryad's Bubble and up the spruce path to Orchard Slope, to ask Diana to tea. As a result, just after Marilla had driven off to Carmody, Diana came over, dressed in *her* second best dress and looking exactly as it is proper to look when asked out to tea. At other times she was wont to run into the kitchen without knocking; but now she knocked primly at the front door. And when Anne, dressed in her second best, as primly opened it, both little girls shook hands as gravely as if they had never met before. This unnatural solemnity lasted until after Diana had been taken to the east gable to lay off her hat and then had sat for ten minutes in the sitting room, toes in position.

"How is your mother?" inquired Anne politely, just as if she had not seen Mrs. Barry picking apples that morning in excellent health and spirits.

"She is very well, thank you. I suppose Mr. Cuthbert is hauling potatoes to the *Lily Sands* this afternoon, is he?" said Diana, who had ridden down to Mr. Harmon Andrews' that morning in Matthew's cart.

"Yes. Our potato crop is very good this year. I hope your father's potato crop is good, too."

"It is fairly good, thank you. Have you picked many of your apples yet?"

"Oh, ever so many," said Anne, forgetting to be dignified and jumping up quickly. "Let's go out to the orchard and get some of the Red Sweetings, Diana. Marilla says we can have all that are left on the tree."

L.M. Montgomery
ANNE OF GREEN GABLES

It was a small but very comfortable and sunny room that Mrs. Wickett let to him. The house itself was ugly and pretentious; but that didn't matter. It was convenient — that was the main thing. For he liked, if the weather were mild enough, to stroll across to the playing fields in an afternoon and watch the games. He liked to smile and exchange a few words with the boys when they touched their caps to him. He made a special point of getting to know all the new boys and having them to tea with him during their first term. He always ordered a walnut cake with pink icing from Reddaway's, in the village, and during the winter term there were crumpets, too — a little pile of them in front of the fire, soaked in butter so that the bottom one lay in a little shallow pool. His guests found it fun to watch him make tea — mixing careful spoonfuls from different caddies. And he would ask the new boys where they lived, and if they had family connections at Brookfield. He kept watch to see that their plates were never empty, and punctually at five, after the session had lasted an hour, he would glance at the clock and say: "Well — umph — it's been very delightful — umph — meeting you like this — I'm sorry — umph — you can't stay . . ." And he would smile and shake hands with them in the porch, leaving them to race across the road to the School with their comments. "Decent old boy, Chips. Gives you a jolly good tea, anyhow, and you *do* know when he wants you to push off . . ."

. . . So there he lived, at Mrs. Wickett's, with his quiet enjoyments of reading and talking and remembering; an old man, white-haired and only a little bald, still fairly active for his years, drinking tea, receiving callers, busying himself with corrections for the next edition of the Brookfeldian Directory, writing his occasional letters in thin, spidery, but very legible script. He had new masters to tea, as well as new boys. There were two of them that autumn term, and as they were leaving after their visit one of them commented: "Quite a character, the old boy, isn't he? All that fuss about mixing tea . . ."

James Hilton
GOOD-BYE MR. CHIPS

friend of mine who grew up alongside a samovar has only one way to describe proper water for tea: "A *mad* boil." In the same forceful way she never says rolls or toast must be hot, or very hot. They must be "hot-hot-*hot!*" This is pronounced as much as possible like a one-syllable sound of intense excitement, about no matter how dull a bun.

. . . The quaint old fiction of the kettle simmering all day on the hearth, waiting to be turned into a delicious cup of tea, is actively disturbing to anyone who cares very much whether his tea will be made from lively water instead of a liquid which is flat, exhausted, tasteless — in other words, with the hell cooked out of it. (Altitude changes the sound, as well as the speed, of boiling water. There seems to be more noise, high up.)

It is safe to say that when the water boils, as it surely will, given enough heat under it, it is ready. Then, at that moment and no other, pour it into the teapot . . . If it cannot be used then, turn off the heat and start over again when you yourself are ready; it will harm you less to wait than it will the water to boil too long.

M. F. K. Fisher
THE ART OF EATING

The hot water is to remain upon the tea no longer than whiles you can say the Miserere Psalm very leisurely.

Sir Kenelm Digby
THE CLOSET OPENED

Sassafras wood boiled down to a kind of tea, and tempered with an infusion of milk and sugar, hath to some a delicacy beyond the China luxury.

Charles Lamb
THE PRAISE OF CHIMNEY-SWEEPERS

THE RECIPES AND MENUS

*A*fternoon Tea
should be provided, fresh supplies, with thin bread-
and-butter, fancy pastries, cakes, etc., being brought in
as other guests arrive.

Mrs. Beeton
THE BOOK OF HOUSEHOLD MANAGEMENT

THE RECIPES AND MENUS

One of the most delightful aspects of the Victorian tea is its balance of sweet and savory. The British are well known for their love of mustard, vinegar, and herbs, which in the form of savories are just the thing to accompany the ultra-rich sweets. It is wonderful to rely on tradition when it comes to menu choices. Cream cakes, warm scones, madeleines, jam tarts, and tiny sandwiches with slivered ham are all in the Victorian mode, made from recipes that cannot be improved upon. A few continental liberties can be taken, such as salmon mousse or fancy puff pastries, but you can stay truly British and never run out of new menu ideas, for the variety is both prolific and delicious.

Tea sandwiches are little bites of fresh flavors that never overwhelm the tea itself. Classics are thinly sliced cucumbers and watercress. The English loaf is never too sweet, and square, flat topped with a small crumb and close texture. Its crusts are always removed. (They can be toasted and used for bread crumbs.) Butter is sweet, not salted, and often delicately flavored with herbs like basil or sage.

When you plan your menu, take the season into consideration. This will dictate whether you will serve hot or iced tea, and the kinds of fruits you can use fresh in recipes like Country Peach and Plum Tart, or Blackberry Tarts. A cold and snowy February inspires Black Walnut Linzer Hearts and piping hot Currant Scones with Smoked Turkey. Select seasonal ingredients whenever possible. All produce tastes superior when it is grown close to home rather than halfway around the world.

A WORD ABOUT INGREDIENTS

As well as perfectly ripe seasonal fruits and berries, we suggest choosing only the finest ingredients for all the recipes. When developing the recipes, we used large grade A eggs, unsalted butter, and pure vanilla extract. If a recipe calls for already baked bread, buy the best at the local bakery or market. Buy nuts in the shells from specialty markets or natural food stores; these are fresher than those in the cellophane-wrapped packets sold in supermarkets. We recommend freshly squeezed lemon juice rather then bottled, and fresh herbs when possible. In our recipes, "sugar" always means granulated unless specified otherwise.

Bake the sweets and make the savory dishes as close to serving time as possible. In the recipes, we have provided storing information when appropriate. You can make tea sandwiches, for instance, several hours before tea, keeping them fresh under a damp tea towel. Many cakes and quick breads mellow and actually taste better if made a day or so ahead of time. Scones and muffins are best served as soon after baking as possible, and pancakes and waffles do not tolerate storage.

BREWING THE PERFECT POT OF TEA

Much has been written about brewing tea. The consensus is that a good pot of tea requires three elements: pure water (the softer the better), *boiling* water, and loose tea (although tea bags, in a pinch, will do!).

To begin, put cold water on to boil in the kettle (this of course should be metal). Cold, running water (not iced) is fully oxygenated and better for tea. If your tap water is very hard or poor tasting, use bottled water. Fill a porcelain teapot with hot tap water and let it sit to warm up while the kettle boils. Just before the water reaches the boil, empty the teapot, dry it, and add the tea. The rule of thumb is one heaping teaspoon of tea for each cup, and then one more "for the pot." If you are using tea bags, use one for each serving and one more for the pot. Set the teapot next to the stove and the moment the water boils, pour it over the tea. It is important that the water be boiling as fully as possible; if you carry the teakettle across the room, the water may drop a degree or two in the few seconds this journey takes. Equally important is that the water not boil too long. If it has been boiling for several minutes or more, not only will you lose much of it to steam, but the water will lose oxygen and the tea not taste as good. Let the tea steep for three to five minutes. Stir it once during steeping to distribute the essential oils. Steeping draws the tannin from the leaves; too much steeping will result in bitter tea. The strength of the tea depends as much on the amount used as on the steeping time. Finally, strain the tea into another warm teapot or directly into cups for serving.

Whatever the occasion, giving a tea party allows you the opportunity to entertain good friends and kind acquaintances with sweet style. Take care with the food, brew a bracing pot of tea, but most importantly, enjoy the warmth and joy possible only when gentle people gather for a lovely party.

TEAS

Mint Tea

The smoky flavor of China tea is perfectly complemented by bits of fresh mint leaves. Add sugar, if you desire, and lemon slices and mint sprigs for a bit more flavor and color.

YIELD: 4 servings

3 teaspoons China tea
¼ cup chopped fresh mint
3½ to 4 cups boiling water
4 lemon slices and mint sprigs
4 to 5 teaspoons sugar, optional

1.   Warm a teapot and teacups with hot water. Drain and dry them.
2.   Combine the tea leaves and chopped mint in the teapot. Add the boiling water. Cover with a tea towel or tea cozy and steep for 5 minutes.
3.   Stir and strain into the hot cups, and garnish with lemon slices and mint sprigs. Serve right away, with or without the sugar.

Orange-Clove Tea

The marriage of orange-pekoe with spicy cloves and sweet fresh oranges can warm the weary soul on a gray winter's day. For extra flavor, slip one or two clove-studded orange slices into the pot while the tea is brewing.

YIELD: 4 servings

3 to 4 teaspoons orange-pekoe tea
1 quart boiling water
1 orange, rinsed, dried, and cut into slices about
   ½-inch thick
Whole cloves

1.   Warm a teapot and teacups with hot water. Drain and dry them.
2.   Put the tea leaves in the teapot. Add the boiling water. Cover with a tea towel or tea cozy and steep for 5 minutes.
3.   Cut each orange slice in half, so that each piece is a semi-circle. Stud the skin side with several whole cloves. Put an orange slice in the bottom of each teacup.
4.   Stir and strain the tea into the hot cups and serve.

Lovers' Tea

46

Lovers' Tea

What a pretty picture: freshly brewed tea poured into dainty teacups and decorated with floating rose petals. The rose petals may be from the dozen long-stems delivered that afternoon, or perhaps they were recently cut from rose bushes in the garden. The tea is a personal blend you make yourself and keep stored in a tin, to bring out when the occasion merits something special.

YIELD: 16 to 20 servings

1 cup loose jasmine tea leaves
1 tablespoon dried lavender flowers
1 teaspoon dried marjoram
¼ cup dried rose petals
32 to 40 fresh, pesticide-free rose petals
  (2 for each cup)

TO MAKE THE DRIED TEA MIXTURE:
1.   In a medium bowl, combine the tea leaves, lavender flowers, marjoram, and dried rose petals.
2.   Transfer the mixture to a container with a tight-fitting lid and store it in a cool, dark place.

TO MAKE THE TEA:
1.   Warm a teapot and teacups with hot water. Drain and dry them.
2.   For each cup of tea, put 1 tablespoon of the tea mixture and ¾ cup boiling water into the teapot. Cover with a tea towel or tea cozy and steep for 5 minutes.
3.   Stir the tea and strain it into the cups.
4.   Remove the bitter white heel from each rose petal. Crush the petals slightly to release their flavor and then gently float 2 petals on the surface of each cup of tea. Serve right away.

Vanilla Milk Tea

This sweet, milky tea gives children a perfect introduction to our favorite. The large share of milk in each cup can be reduced for older members of the party who may prefer a bit more tea. Try this, too, on a stormy day — it soothes and comforts as few other beverages do. Do use a vanilla bean if at all possible. If not, stir 2 teaspoons of pure vanilla extract into the milk.

YIELD: 4 to 5 servings

1 cup milk
1 2-inch piece of vanilla bean, split
4 teaspoons English Breakfast tea
1 quart boiling water

1.   Pour the milk in a small saucepan, add the vanilla bean, and bring to a simmer, stirring often. Remove the pan from the heat and let it stand until the milk is cool. Remove the bean.
2.   Warm a teapot and teacups with hot water. Drain and dry them.
3.   Put the tea leaves in the teapot and add the boiling water. Cover with a tea towel or cozy and steep for 5 minutes.
4.   Pour about ¼ cup of the cooled milk into the teacups.
5.   Stir and strain the tea into the hot cups. Serve right away.

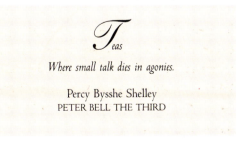

Teas

Where small talk dies in agonies.

Percy Bysshe Shelley
PETER BELL THE THIRD

Lemon-Mint Tea

Lemon and mint are a classic combination. Try the tea iced with Lime Wafers (page 72) or Lemon Bread (page 57).

YIELD: 6 to 8 servings

2 quarts water
2 tablespoons lemon tea
2 teaspoons mint tea
6 to 8 lemon slices

1.   In a large saucepan, bring the water to a full boil. Add the tea either loose or in a fine mesh infuser. Cover and let the tea stand for 5 minutes.
2.   Strain and cool to room temperature.
3.   Serve the tea over ice, garnished with the lemon slices.

Orange-Spice Tea

Fragrant orange-pekoe tea is enhanced when it is infused with a cinnamon stick and a pod of star anise, which tastes of licorice.

YIELD: 6 to 8 servings

2 quarts water
8 teaspoons loose orange-pekoe tea
½ cup sugar
1 stick cinnamon
1 pod star anise
6 to 8 quartered orange slices

1.   In a large saucepan, bring the water to a full boil. Add the tea, sugar, cinnamon, and star anise. Cover and let the tea stand for 5 minutes.
2.   Strain and cool to room temperature.
3.   Serve the tea over ice, garnished with the orange slices.

Strawberry Tea

Strawberry tea, which contains no caffeine and is easy to locate in specialty shops, natural-food stores, and many supermarkets, is an especially appealing iced drink. You might serve it in June, bejeweled with strawberries at their height — plump, juicy, and deep glistening red.

YIELD: 6 to 8 servings

2 quarts water
8 teaspoons strawberry tea
½ cup sugar
Juice of 1 lemon
About 4 strawberries, sliced

1.   In a large saucepan, bring the water to a full boil. Add the tea and sugar, cover, and let stand for 5 minutes.
2.   Strain the tea into a large pot or pan. Stir in the lemon juice, and let the tea cool to room temperature.
3.   Serve the tea over ice, garnished with the sliced strawberries.

A Cozy Tea for Two

Currant and Pecan Scones

Grilled Marmalade Fingers

Meringue Kisses

Lemon Ginger Pound Cake

Berry-Flavored Honey

Orange-Spice Tea

Iced Clove Cooler

The bold flavors of cloves and cardamom and the sweet ones of ginger and allspice make a surprisingly piquant iced drink. Serve this at a tea where much of the food is savory.

YIELD: 6 to 8 servings

2 quarts water
16 whole cloves
5 cardamom seeds (preferably green), crushed
1 tablespoon crystallized ginger, chopped
1/4 teaspoon whole allspice
6 to 8 lemon slices and mint sprigs

1. In a large saucepan, bring the water to a full boil. Add the cloves, cardamom, ginger, and allspice. Cover and let the tea stand for 7 minutes.
2. Strain the tea and let it cool to room temperature.
3. Serve the tea over ice, with lemon slices and sprigs of fresh mint.

Lavender and Lime

We can't imagine a more refreshing iced summer drink than this blending of fragrant lavender and tangy lime. And it looks so pretty poured into tall, frosty glasses.

YIELD: 5 servings

3 tablespoons crushed fresh lavender flowers,
  or 1 tablespoon dried lavender flowers
1 cup boiling water
1 6-ounce can frozen limeade concentrate
5 lavender flower sprigs

1. Place the lavender flowers in a small teapot or bowl. Pour the boiling water over the flowers. Steep, covered, for at least 10 minutes, or until cool.
2. While the tea is cooling, prepare the limeade according to the package directions.
3. Stir and strain the tea into the limeade. Serve over ice, with the flower sprigs.

Ginger Pear Delight

Serving ginger-flavored sweets was common in Victorian times. Here, ginger is steeped in boiling water to yield a mildly flavored drink that blends nicely with rich fruit nectar.

YIELD: 5 servings

2 tablespoons thinly sliced fresh ginger
1/2 cup boiling water
2 cups pear, peach, or apricot nectar
2 cups club soda, chilled
5 pear, peach, or apricot slices, dipped in freshly
  squeezed lemon juice

1. Put the ginger in a small teapot or bowl. Pour the boiling water over it and let it steep, covered, for about 10 minutes, or until cool. Strain and mix the cooled ginger liquid with the fruit nectar.
2. For each serving, pour 1/2 cup of the ginger-nectar mixture over ice in a glass. Add about 1/3 cup of chilled club soda. Stir gently and garnish with the sliced fruit.

Your very Chambermaids have lost their bloom, I suppose by sipping tea.

Unknown English writer
1757

Rosy Yogurt Cooler

Rosy Yogurt Cooler

A berry-filled yogurt shake may appeal to anyone who is not overly fond of plain tea but wants a smooth and tasty drink to sip. Depending on the size of your blender, you may have to make this in several batches. Serve the frothy drink in tall glasses.

YIELD: 4 servings

2 rosehip tea bags
2 cups boiling water
2 cups plain lowfat yogurt
1 cup sliced strawberries, blueberries, or raspberries
3 tablespoons honey
About 8 strawberries, blueberries, or raspberries

1.   Put the rosehip tea bags in a small teapot or bowl. Pour the boiling water over them and let them steep, covered, for about 10 minutes. Remove the tea bags.
2.   Put the yogurt, berries, and honey in a blender. Blend until smooth.
3.   Add the tea to the yogurt mixture. Blend until smooth.
4.   Serve over ice, with whole berries.

Double Lemon Punch

Gently flavored with lemon-verbena leaves or lemon tea, this ginger ale-based punch is a pretty addition to the tea table. Children will like it too, and guests will be charmed by the flowery ice cubes. You may want to make some extra cubes to replenish the punch.

YIELD: 8 to 10 servings

Floral Ice:
16 to 24 small edible flowers such as borage, sage, lavender, rose petals, or rose buds, or 10 to 14 large edible flowers such as calendula or nasturtium

Punch:
½ cup fresh lemon-verbena leaves, or 3 tablespoons dried leaves, or 2 lemon tea bags
2 cups boiling water
2 cups black tea, cooled
Juice of 2 lemons
1 quart ginger ale, chilled

TO MAKE THE FLORAL ICE:
1.   Gently wash the flowers and place 1 or 2 small ones in each compartment of an ice tray. Add water in a soft stream and freeze.
2.   Or, for a larger block of ice, use an 8- or 9-inch cake pan. Scatter the large flowers, blossom side down in the cake pan, or mix them with some smaller blooms. Add ⅛ inch of cold water. Freeze until firm, about 1 hour. Fill the cake pan almost full with cold water. Freeze for 5 hours or until frozen. Dip the pan in hot water to loosen the ice block.

TO MAKE AND SERVE THE PUNCH:
1.   Place the lemon-verbena leaves or lemon tea bags in a small teapot or bowl. Pour boiling water over them and let the

mixture steep, covered, for at least 10 minutes. Strain or remove the tea bags.

2. In a large punch bowl, mix the cooled lemon tea, cooled black tea, and lemon juice. Cover and refrigerate until serving time, or for at least 30 minutes.

3. Just before serving, add the ginger ale. Stir gently to mix. Float the floral ice in the punch.

White Winter Champagne Punch

This is an elegant punch for a fancy tea. The wine and port combine with bubbling champagne, to be ladled from a crystal punch bowl into the pretty sugar-iced glasses. Lemon-verbena leaves give off a pleasing lemon scent and may be used to make a wreath to encircle the punch bowl.

YIELD: 12 to 15 servings

Lemon-Verbena Sugar:
1 cup lemon-verbena leaves
2 cups superfine sugar

Punch:
2 cups lemon-flavored mineral water
1 cup superfine sugar
½ cup lemon-verbena leaves
1 (750 ml) bottle white burgundy, chilled
1 (750 ml) bottle white port, chilled
3 (750 ml) bottles brut champagne, chilled
3 lemons, for glasses
12 to 15 lemon-verbena leaves

TO PREPARE THE SUGAR:

From a week to a month ahead, mix the lemon-verbena leaves with the sugar. Store in a tightly covered container, shaking occasionally to mix.

Double Lemon Punch

TO MAKE THE PUNCH:

1. The day before serving, boil the mineral water and superfine sugar for 5 minutes to make a simple syrup. Remove from the heat and make an infusion by adding the lemon-verbena leaves. Cover and let the infusion sit at room temperature overnight.

2. Just before serving, mix the infusion with the chilled burgundy and port in a punch bowl. Slowly pour the chilled champagne down the side of the bowl and stir.

TO PREPARE THE GLASSES AND SERVE:

1. Cut the lemons into wedges. Rub the lemon wedges over the inside of saucer-shaped champagne glasses and ½-inch of the outside rim of each glass.

2. In a shallow bowl, pie plate, or saucer, spoon the lemon-verbena sugar so that it is about an inch deep. Dip the rim of each glass in the sugar. Sprinkle some into the glass and swirl to coat. Repeat for each glass.

3. Chill the glasses in the refrigerator for at least 30 minutes, or in the freezer for at least 15 minutes, or until serving time.

4. When it is time to serve, ladle the punch into the sugar-frosted glasses and garnish with lemon-verbena leaves.

SAVORIES

Watercress Sandwiches

As the custom of taking afternoon tea gained in popularity during the last century, the array of delicate morsels served with the hot drink got more elaborate. Soon sweets accompanied the buttered bread and muffins, and then came tea sandwiches made from very fine white bread and light-tasting ingredients such as watercress, tomatoes, cucumbers, and chopped egg. If you make the sandwiches ahead of time, keep them covered with a damp, well-wrung tea towel.

YIELD: 12 sandwiches

Ham-Watercress Sandwiches:
2 thin slices white bread, crusts removed
2 tablespoons cream cheese with chives, softened
2 thin slices baked ham
1/3 cup small watercress sprigs, thick stems removed
12 orange sections
2 teaspoons minced red onion

1. Spread the slices of bread with the cream cheese.
2. Trim the ham to fit the slices of bread. Layer the ham and watercress on the bread. Using a serrated knife, cut the sandwich in half diagonally.
3. Garnish the sandwiches with orange sections and sprinkle with red onion.

Chicken-Watercress Sandwiches:
2 slices thin white bread, crusts removed
2 tablespoons cream cheese with chives, softened
4 thin slices cooked chicken breast
1/3 cup watercress sprigs, thick stems removed
12 thin cucumber slices
4 strips pimiento

1. Spread the slices of bread with the cream cheese.
2. Trim the chicken to fit the bread. Layer the chicken and watercress on the bread. With a serrated knife, cut the sandwich in half diagonally.
3. Garnish the sandwiches with the cucumber and pimiento.

Bacon-Watercress Sandwiches:
2 slices thin white bread, crusts removed
2 tablespoons cream cheese with chives, softened
2 slices bacon, cooked and crumbled
1/3 cup small watercress sprigs, thick stems removed
4 avocado slices, brushed with lemon juice
 and halved
Paprika

1. Spread the bread with cream cheese.
2. Top the bread with bacon and watercress. Using a serrated knife, cut the sandwich in half diagonally.
3. Garnish the sandwiches with avocado slices and sprinkle with paprika.

Herbed Cream Cheese Sandwiches

Cream cheese with herbs fresh from your own garden or the local market makes a fine sandwich. You can prepare the cream cheese mixture several hours ahead, but let it come to room temperature before spreading.

YIELD: 16 sandwiches

1 cup (8 ounces) cream cheese, softened
½ cup lightly packed finely chopped fresh herb leaves
  such as parsley, watercress, basil, chervil, or chives,
  by themselves or any combination
1 tablespoon freshly squeezed lemon juice
Dash of bottled hot pepper sauce
8 slices firm-textured wheat bread, crusts removed
Paprika

1. In a small mixing bowl, combine the cream cheese, herbs, lemon juice, and hot pepper sauce. Mix the ingredients well.
2. Spread about 2 tablespoons of the mixture on each bread. Sprinkle with paprika.
3. Put the slices together to make 4 sandwiches. Using a serrated knife, cut them diagonally into quarters.

Cucumber Sandwiches with Mint Butter

Simple and elegant, cucumber sandwiches are the stuff of tea time. With a handful of mint leaves added to the butter, these are especially tasty. Burnet leaves, commonly found in Europe and Asia, are cultivated here for their young, tender leaves, which taste a little like cucumbers. As such, they are perfect for embellishing a plateful of delicate sandwiches.

YIELD: 8 sandwiches

Cucumber Sandwiches with Mint Butter

¼ cup (½ stick) butter, softened
2 tablespoons fresh mint leaves, chopped
8 very thin slices white bread, crusts removed
½ large cucumber, peeled and thinly sliced
Burnet sprigs and ripe black olives

1. In a small bowl, combine the butter and mint. Mix well.
2. Spread the mint butter on the bread slices. Lay the cucumber on 4 of the slices and top with the remaining bread to make 4 sandwiches. Cut them in half diagonally.
3. Place the sandwiches on a serving plate. Add the burnet sprigs and olives.

Stands the church clock at ten to three?

And is there honey still for tea?

Rupert Brooke
HEAVEN

Stilton, Pear, and Watercress Savory

Stilton and pears are a classic combination, for a very good reason. Once you try them together, you will understand why they have been paired for nearly as long as the English have been making their famous blue cheese.

YIELD: 4 servings

4 slices dark rye bread, toasted
1 cup small watercress sprigs, thick stems removed
2 ripe pears, cored and sliced
8 ounces Stilton
Juice of ½ lemon
Freshly ground black pepper
Red-leaf lettuce

1. Preheat the oven to 400°F. Arrange the toast slices in a single layer in a heat-proof dish or a shallow baking pan. Layer the watercress sprigs and half the pear slices over the toast. Crumble the Stilton over the pears. Sprinkle the remaining pear slices with the lemon juice to prevent them from discoloring and set aside.
2. Bake the toast slices for 10 minutes, or until the cheese is melted and bubbling. Grind a little pepper over each. Serve the savory garnished with the red-leaf lettuce and the remaining pear slices.

If one would merely slake his thirst, then he can drink rice and water. Should melancholy, sadness or anger strike, he can turn to drink. But if one would dispel an evening's unproductive lassitude, the meaning of "drink" is tea.

Lu Yu
THE CLASSIC OF TEA

Salmon Mousse

The light, delicate flavor of these individual mousses seems extremely appropriate for late-afternoon tea. If the mousses do not unmold easily, dip them into a bowl of very hot water for just a few seconds.

YIELD: 10 servings

1 envelope unflavored gelatin
¼ cup cold water
½ cup boiling water
½ cup mayonnaise
1 tablespoon grated onion
1 tablespoon freshly squeezed lemon juice
1 teaspoon salt
½ teaspoon paprika
½ teaspoon bottled hot pepper sauce
2 cups drained, flaked salmon
½ cup heavy cream

1. In a medium bowl, sprinkle the gelatin over the cold water. Let it stand for 5 minutes, until it is softened. Add the boiling water and stir until the gelatin dissolves. Let it cool to room temperature.
2. Whisk the mayonnaise, onion, lemon juice, salt, paprika, and hot pepper sauce into the gelatin. Mix well. Cover the bowl and refrigerate for 30 to 60 minutes, or until the mixture is the consistency of unbeaten egg whites.
3. Butter ten ⅓-cup molds.
4. Remove the mixture from the refrigerator and stir in the salmon. Beat well with an electric mixer set at medium speed.
5. In a small bowl, whip the cream until soft peaks form. Fold the whipped cream into the salmon mixture. Fill each of the prepared molds. Cover and refrigerate until set, at least 4 hours.

6. To serve, loosen the edges of the molds with a knife. Invert the molds on a serving plate and, gently shaking each one, lift it off the mousse.

Spinach Cheese Tartlets

The filling for these pretty tartlets is quick and simple to make. The pastry shells, which take a little longer to prepare, may be made ahead of time and stored in the freezer.

YIELD: 30 to 32 tartlets

Pastry:
½ cup (1 stick) cold butter, cut into pieces
6 tablespoons lard
2½ cups all-purpose flour
4 to 6 tablespoons ice water

Filling:
4 eggs
1 ½ cups (12 ounces) cottage cheese
1 small onion, finely chopped
2 garlic cloves, minced
1 10-ounce package frozen chopped spinach, thawed
1 cup shredded Monterey Jack cheese
½ cup freshly grated Parmesan cheese
½ teaspoon salt

TO MAKE THE PASTRY:
1. In a large bowl, cut the butter and lard into the flour with a pastry blender or 2 knives until the mixture resembles coarse crumbs. Sprinkle the ice water over the mixture, 1 tablespoon at a time, stirring with a fork until the pastry is well blended and gathers into a ball. Sprinkle the dough with a little flour. Wrap it in plastic and refrigerate at least 1 hour.
2. Divide the chilled dough into 2 portions. Roll one portion out on a lightly floured work surface into a circle about ⅛-inch thick. Cut out pieces to fit onto 2½- to 3-inch tartlet pans. Gently press the pieces of dough into the pans and prick them on bottom with a fork. Repeat with the second portion of dough. Put the pans on a baking sheet and place them in the freezer for about 15 minutes, or until the dough is firm.
3. Preheat the oven to 375°F. Cut small squares of foil, each about 3 inches square, for each tartlet.
4. Remove the pans from the freezer. Line the pastry with the foil squares, shiny side down, and fill the foil with dried beans, rice, or pastry weights to keep the pastry flat during baking.
5. Bake the pastry shells 12 to 15 minutes, or until the foil lifts out of the shells easily. Remove the foil and weights from the shells. Continue baking the shells 8 to 10 minutes, or until the pastry is very lightly browned and firm. Cool the shells completely, about 45 minutes, in the pans.
6. Remove the cooled shells from the pans. They may be stored in the refrigerator in a tightly closed container for a few days or in the freezer for several weeks.

TO MAKE THE TARTLETS:
1. Preheat the oven to 375°F. In a medium bowl, beat the eggs. Add the cottage cheese, onion, and garlic and mix well.
2. In a sieve, press the water out of the spinach. Add the spinach, cheeses, and salt to the egg mixture. Stir until well mixed.
3. Fill each baked pastry shell with about 2 tablespoons of filling.
4. Put the shells on baking sheets and bake for 20 to 22 minutes, or until they are puffed and golden on top. Serve hot.

BREADS

Sage Bread

It is said that sage, an herb long popular in the Mediterranean countries of Europe, brings prosperity and good health to all who grow it. Interestingly, long ago the Dutch dried sage leaves, much as tea is dried, and traded it with the Chinese for China tea. Today, adding sage to a simple loaf such as this one gives the bread a strong, true flavor that enhances a good cup of tea.

YIELD: One 9-inch loaf

½ cup milk

2 tablespoons chopped fresh sage, or 1 tablespoon dried sage

2 cups all-purpose flour

1 tablespoon baking powder

1 teaspoon salt

½ cup (1 stick) butter, softened

½ cup sugar

2 eggs

1.   Preheat the oven to 350°F. Butter and flour a 9 x 5 x 3-inch loaf pan.

2.   In a small saucepan, combine the milk and sage, and bring almost to a boil over medium heat. Remove the milk mixture from the heat and let it stand until cool.

3.   In a medium bowl, stir together the flour, baking powder, and salt. Set aside.

4.   In the medium bowl of an electric mixer, beat the butter at medium speed to soften. Gradually add the sugar and continue beating until the mixture is light and fluffy, scraping the sides of the bowl often. Add the eggs, one at a time, beating well after each addition.

5.   Strain the milk to remove the sage, if desired. If you do not strain it, the bread will have a more pronounced sage flavor.

6.   Add the flour mixture and milk alternately to the butter mixture, stirring well with a wooden spoon after each addition. Spread the batter evenly in the prepared pan.

7.   Bake the bread for 50 to 60 minutes, or until a toothpick inserted in center of the loaf comes out clean.

8.   Cool the bread in the pan on a wire rack for 10 minutes. Then remove the bread from the pan to cool on the rack.

Andrews the Smuggler brought me this night about 11 o'clock a bag of Hyson Tea 6 Pd weight. He frightened us a little by whistling under the Parlour Window just as we were going to bed. I gave him some Geneva [gin] and paid him for the tea.

Seventeenth-century English diarist

Lemon Bread

Because this bread is made with lemonade, lemon zest, and lemon extract, the flavor is wonderfully intense. We suggest making the lemonade for the bread from frozen concentrate rather than relying on pre-mixed lemonade or that from fresh lemons. The sweet loaf slices easily and requires no accompaniment other than a nice cup of tea.

YIELD: One 9-inch loaf

2 cups all-purpose flour
1 tablespoon baking powder
¼ teaspoon salt
½ cup (1 stick) butter, softened
1 cup sugar
2 eggs
Grated zest of 1 lemon
1 teaspoon lemon extract
¾ cup lemonade

1.   Preheat the oven to 350°F. Butter and flour a 9 x 5 x 3-inch loaf pan. Line the bottom of the pan with wax paper. Butter and flour the wax paper. Shake out excess flour.
2.   In a medium bowl, thoroughly stir together the flour, baking powder, and salt.

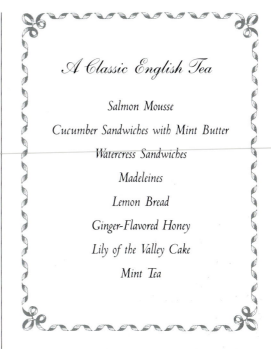

A Classic English Tea

Salmon Mousse

Cucumber Sandwiches with Mint Butter

Watercress Sandwiches

Madeleines

Lemon Bread

Ginger-Flavored Honey

Lily of the Valley Cake

Mint Tea

3.   In the medium bowl of an electric mixer, beat the butter and sugar at medium speed until the mixture is light and fluffy, scraping the sides of the bowl often. Add the eggs, one at a time, beating well after each addition.
4.   Add the lemon zest and lemon extract. With the mixer set at low speed, add the dry ingredients alternately with the lemonade, and mix just until blended. Spread the batter evenly in the prepared pan.
5.   Bake for 60 to 65 minutes, or until a toothpick inserted in the center of the loaf comes out clean.
6.   Cool the bread in the pan on a wire rack for 10 minutes. Then remove from the pan, peel off the wax paper, and let the bread cool completely on the rack.

Lemon Thyme Bread (page 58)

Lemon Thyme Bread

Lemon thyme has a noticeable and extremely pleasant lemony tang. In this quick loaf, it not only adds bright lemon flavor but makes the bread especially attractive as it flecks the crumb with a little green.

YIELD: One 9-inch loaf

2 cups all-purpose flour
2 teaspoons baking powder
¼ teaspoon salt
6 tablespoons (¾ stick) butter, softened
1 cup sugar
2 eggs
1 tablespoon grated lemon zest
2 tablespoons freshly squeezed lemon juice
2 tablespoons finely chopped lemon thyme
⅔ cup milk
2 tablespoons freshly squeezed lemon juice, for glaze
½ cup sifted confectioners' sugar, for glaze

1. Preheat the oven to 350°F. Butter and flour a 9 x 5 x 3-inch loaf pan.
2. In a medium bowl, sift together the flour, baking powder, and salt. Set aside.
3. In the medium bowl of an electric mixer, beat the butter and sugar at medium speed until the mixture is light and fluffy, scraping the sides of the bowl often. Add the eggs, one at a time, beating well after each addition.
4. Beat in the lemon zest, lemon juice, and lemon thyme. With the mixer at low speed, add the dry ingredients alternately with the milk, and mix just until blended. Spread the batter in the prepared pan.
5. Bake for 55 to 60 minutes, or until a toothpick inserted in the center of the loaf comes out clean. Cool the baked bread in the pan on a wire rack for 10 minutes.
6. While the bread is cooling, make a glaze. In a small bowl, mix the lemon juice and enough confectioners' sugar for a thin, pourable consistency.
7. Turn the bread out onto a wire rack positioned over a sheet of paper. Slowly pour the glaze over the bread.

Pumpkin Nut Bread

The whole-wheat pastry flour adds a satisfying nutty flavor to this moist pumpkin bread while maintaining a fine-crumbed texture. You can find whole-wheat pastry flour in health-food stores, or you can use triple-sifted whole-wheat flour. This will make the bread a little more densely textured.

YIELD: Two 9-inch loaves

1 cup (2 sticks) butter, softened
2 cups packed dark-brown sugar
4 eggs
1 16-ounce can pumpkin puree, or 2 cups fresh
  pumpkin, cooked and mashed
⅓ cup molasses
2 cups all-purpose flour
2 cups whole-wheat pastry flour
1 tablespoon baking powder
1 teaspoon ground cinnamon
1 teaspoon salt
½ teaspoon baking soda
½ teaspoon freshly grated nutmeg
1½ cups toasted slivered almonds or chopped walnuts

1. Preheat the oven to 350°F. Butter two 9 x 5 x 3-inch loaf pans.
2. In the large mixing bowl of an electric mixer, cream the butter and brown sugar at medium speed until the mixture is fluffy,

scraping the sides of the bowl often. Beat in the eggs, then the pumpkin and molasses. The mixture will look curdled. Set aside.

3.   In another large bowl, thoroughly mix the remaining ingredients except the nuts.

4.   With the mixer set at low, gradually beat the dry mixture into the pumpkin mixture, just until blended. Stir in the nuts. Pour the batter into the prepared pans.

5.   Bake for 60 to 65 minutes or until a toothpick inserted in the center of a loaf comes out clean.

6.   Cool the bread in the pans on wire racks for 10 minutes. Remove the loaves from the pans and let them cool completely on the racks.

Milk and Honey Bread with Honey Butter

Few cups of tea are more comforting than those sweetened with a little milk and honey — and nothing tastes better with the tea than a thick slice of sweet honey bread, rich with its own honey butter. Try this satisfying combination when the occasion calls for something warm and soothing.

YIELD: One 9-inch loaf

1 cup milk
½ cup honey
3 tablespoons butter, melted
2½ cups all-purpose flour
½ cup sugar
1 tablespoon baking powder
1 teaspoon salt
¾ cup chopped pecans
1 egg

Honey Butter:
½ cup (1 stick) butter, softened
½ cup honey
2 tablespoons heavy cream

TO MAKE THE BREAD:

1.   Preheat the oven to 375°F. Butter a 9 x 5 x 3-inch loaf pan.

2.   In a medium saucepan, combine the milk and honey. Stir over medium heat until the honey dissolves. Stir in the melted butter. Set aside to cool.

3.   In a large bowl, sift together the flour, sugar, baking powder, and salt. Add the pecans and toss to mix. Set the mixture aside.

4.   Pour the cooled milk mixture into the large bowl of an electric mixer and beat in the egg. When it is well blended, add the flour mixture. With the mixer at medium speed, beat just until the ingredients are blended. Spread the batter evenly in the prepared pan.

5.   Turn down the oven to 350°F and bake the bread for 65 to 70 minutes, or until a toothpick inserted in the center of the loaf comes out clean.

6.   Cool the bread in the pan on a wire rack for 10 minutes. Remove it from the pan and let it cool completely on the rack.

TO MAKE THE BUTTER:

1.   In the medium bowl of an electric mixer, beat the butter at medium speed to soften. Beat in the honey until blended.

2.   Gradually beat in the cream until the mixture is smooth and creamy. Serve at room temperature.

Cinnamon Raisin Roll-Ups

This variation on old-fashioned cinnamon toast looks especially pretty arranged pinwheel-style on a plain crockery plate. Offer these on a cold evening with Vanilla Milk Tea (page 47) or a mug of hot chocolate.

YIELD: 12 roll-ups

12 thin slices white bread
6 tablespoons (¾ stick) butter, softened
½ cup sugar
1½ tablespoons cinnamon
½ cup raisins, approximately

1.   Preheat the oven to 300°F. Cut the crusts from the bread. Gently roll out each slice with a rolling pin to make it thinner and more flexible.
2.   In a medium bowl, cream the butter and sugar, and then stir in the cinnamon. Divide the butter mixture equally among the 12 slices of bread and spread it over the surface of each.
3.   Arrange a row of raisins along one edge of each slice of bread. Starting with this edge, roll each slice jelly-roll style. Fasten with a toothpick, if necessary.
4.   Place the roll-ups on an unbuttered baking sheet, seam side down, and toast in the oven until they are slightly browned, turning occasionally to brown all sides. Serve warm.

United Methodist

Improved Hot Muffin and Crumpet Baking and

Punctual Delivery Company

Charles Dickens
NICHOLAS NICKLEBY

Heavenly Hots

These sweet little pancakes are simply dressed with a sprinkling of confectioners' sugar and a squeeze of lemon juice, then drizzled with Blackberry Syrup (page 68) or spread with Spiced Blackberry Jam (page 68). Whatever your pleasure, make them just before serving time so that they come to the table piping hot and fresh off the griddle.

YIELD: Fifty to sixty 2½-inch pancakes

4 eggs
5 tablespoons cake flour
3 tablespoons sugar
1 teaspoon baking soda
½ teaspoon salt
2 cups sour cream
Butter or vegetable oil

1.   Place the eggs in a blender or a food processor. Add the flour, sugar, baking soda, and salt, and blend or process until the mixture is smooth.
2.   Spoon in the sour cream and process again until smooth.
3.   Heat a griddle or a heavy skillet brushed with butter or vegetable oil. When it is hot, drop a 1-tablespoon measure of batter onto the griddle for each 2½-inch round. (Do not attempt to make larger hot cakes; they will be too fragile to turn.)
4.   Cook each one for 40 to 50 seconds, until a few bubbles appear on top, and then carefully turn and cook the other side of each for 20 to 30 seconds, until the pancakes are golden brown. Serve immediately, if possible, or keep the pancakes warm by covering them with foil and putting them in the oven set at a low temperature while you cook the remaining batter.

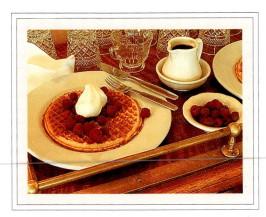

Raised Waffles

Raised Waffles

A little planning is necessary for these airy waffles since the batter must be mixed hours before cooking to give the yeast time to perform its magic. The recipe however, is fairly easy; for more richness, sprinkle a handful of toasted pecans over the batter on the hot waffle iron. If you are feeling particularly indulgent, choose fresh sweet raspberries and whipped cream to complete the dish.

YIELD: 4 to 5 large waffles

½ cup warm water (105° to 115°F)
1 package active dry yeast
2 cups warm milk (105° to 115°F)
½ cup (1 stick) butter, melted
1 teaspoon salt
1 teaspoon sugar
2 cups all-purpose flour
2 eggs
¼ teaspoon baking soda

1.   Pour the warm water into a 3-quart mixing bowl. Sprinkle the yeast over the water, stir, and let the mixture stand 5 minutes, until the yeast dissolves and the mixture bubbles and foams. Stir well.

2.   Add the milk, butter, salt, and sugar. Mix well. Gradually add the flour, mixing until smooth and blended.

3.   Cover the bowl with plastic wrap and let the batter stand overnight at room temperature. (Be sure the bowl is at least 4 times the volume of the batter so that it will not overflow during rising.)

4.   Prepare the waffle iron according to the manufacturer's directions. Preheat to the highest setting.

5.   Just before cooking, beat the eggs and then the baking soda into the batter and mix well. The batter will be thin.

6.   Fill the iron with batter and bake each waffle until the steaming stops and it is a golden brown. (These waffles will take twice as long to cook as conventional ones.)

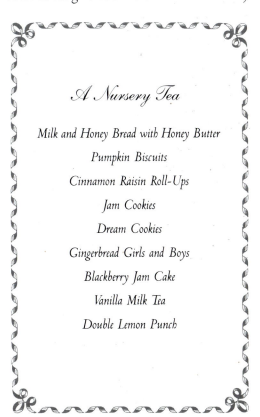

A Nursery Tea

Milk and Honey Bread with Honey Butter

Pumpkin Biscuits

Cinnamon Raisin Roll-Ups

Jam Cookies

Dream Cookies

Gingerbread Girls and Boys

Blackberry Jam Cake

Vanilla Milk Tea

Double Lemon Punch

Pumpkin Biscuits

Whole-wheat flour and pumpkin puree produce substantial biscuits that taste just right
with a hearty tea.

YIELD: About 16 biscuits

1 cup all-purpose flour
1 cup whole-wheat pastry flour
2 tablespoons packed dark-brown sugar
1 tablespoon baking powder
1 teaspoon pumpkin-pie spice
1 teaspoon salt
½ cup (1 stick) cold butter, cut into 8 pieces
1 8-ounce can pumpkin puree, or 1 cup fresh
  pumpkin, cooked and mashed
2 tablespoons heavy cream

1. Preheat the oven to 450°F.
2. In a food processor, combine both
flours, the brown sugar, baking powder,
pumpkin-pie spice, and salt. Process until
the mixture is blended.
3. Distribute the butter evenly over the
flour mixture in the processor. Pulse the
processor on and off until the butter is the
size of peas.
4. Spoon the pumpkin puree evenly over
the flour mixture, still in the bowl of the
processor. Process until the dough begins to
come together but has not yet formed a
ball. The dough should be soft. Do not
overprocess it or the biscuits will be tough.
5. On a lightly floured board, pat out the
dough with floured fingers to make a
9-inch-diameter circle about ½-inch thick.
With a floured 2-inch biscuit cutter or upturned glass, cut out biscuits.
6. Place the biscuit rounds on an unbuttered baking sheet. Brush each lightly with

Pumpkin Nut Bread (page 58) and
Pumpkin Biscuits

cream. With a fork, prick the top of each
biscuit twice.
7. Bake for 12 to 14 minutes, or until the
biscuits are lightly browned. Serve warm.

Blackberry Muffin Miniatures

These tiny, berry-filled muffins are delicious
mouthfuls of summertime. Use just-picked
berries, if you can, or buy them from a farm
stand. Raspberries or boysenberries are wonderful for this recipe as well. If you choose
cultivated boysenberries, cut them in half before adding them to the batter.

YIELD: About 20 small muffins

1 cup all-purpose flour
⅓ cup sugar
1½ teaspoons baking powder
Pinch of salt
1 egg yolk
6 tablespoons milk
3 tablespoons butter, melted
1½ cups fresh blackberries

1.   Preheat the oven to 450°F. Line 20 or more miniature muffin cups measuring 1¼ inches across with paper baking cups.

2.   In a medium bowl, stir together the flour, sugar, baking powder, and salt. Set the mixture aside.

3.   In another medium bowl, lightly whisk the egg yolk. Whisk in the milk, then the butter. Quickly stir in the dry ingredients, stirring only until they are moistened. The batter will be a little lumpy. Fold in the berries. Spoon the batter into the prepared muffin cups, filling them so that the batter is almost level with the rim.

4.   Bake for 9 to 11 minutes, or until a toothpick inserted in the center of a muffin comes out clean.

5.   Cool in the pan for 1 minute. Remove the muffins from the pan and serve hot.

6.   Repeat the baking procedure with any remaining batter. If there is not enough batter to fill all the muffin cups, put water in the empty ones during baking.

Currant and Pecan Scones

Currant and Pecan Scones

Scones are as expected on the tea table as the teapot itself. Quintessential examples are these, made with currants and pecans. Traditional companions for scones are some sweet butter, or a dollop of Devonshire or softly beaten cream.

YIELD: 24 scones

3½ cups all-purpose flour
2 teaspoons baking soda
½ teaspoon salt
½ cup (1 stick) butter, softened
1 cup dried currants or chopped raisins
½ cup finely chopped pecans
1½ cups half-and-half
2 tablespoons sugar
1 teaspoon ground cinnamon

1.   Preheat the oven to 400°F. Butter 2 baking sheets.

2.   In a large bowl, stir together the flour, baking soda, and salt. With 2 knives or a pastry blender, cut the butter into the flour mixture until it resembles coarse crumbs. Stir in the fruit and the pecans. Make a well in the center of the mixture and add the half-and-half. Stir gently with a fork to make a soft, cohesive dough.

3.   Turn the dough out onto a well-floured surface and knead it 10 to 12 times. Roll the dough into a ¼-inch thickness. Cut the dough into rounds using a 2-inch floured biscuit cutter or an upturned floured glass.

4.   In a small bowl, combine the sugar and cinnamon. Arrange the scones, a ½-inch apart, on the prepared baking sheets. Sprinkle the scones with the sugar mixture.

5.   Bake the scones for 10 to 12 minutes, or until they are golden brown. Serve warm.

Currant Scones with Smoked Turkey

Currant Scones with Smoked Turkey

Small scones, split in two and filled with delectable smoked turkey and a bit of piquant apple jelly glaze, are a perfect, if slightly uncommon, combination.

YIELD: 12 to 14 scones

2 cups all-purpose flour
1 teaspoon cream of tartar
½ teaspoon baking soda
Pinch of salt
¼ cup vegetable shortening or margarine
⅓ cup currants
¼ cup milk
¼ cup water

Apple Tarragon Glaze:
⅓ cup apple jelly
2 teaspoons chopped fresh tarragon, or ½ teaspoon dried tarragon
2 teaspoons freshly squeezed lemon juice

Filling:
Butter, softened
1½ pounds thinly sliced smoked turkey

TO MAKE THE SCONES:

1.   Preheat the oven to 450°F. In a large bowl, sift together the flour, cream of tartar, baking soda, and salt. With a pastry blender or 2 knives, cut the shortening into the mixture until it resembles coarse meal. Toss the currants with the flour mixture.

2.   In a 1-cup measuring cup, combine the milk and water. Slowly add the liquid to the flour mixture, mixing with a fork until a soft, pliable dough forms.

3.   On a lightly floured surface, knead the dough gently with floured fingertips to form a smooth dough. Roll the dough out to a ½-inch thickness.

4.   Cut out small hearts or other shapes, using cookie cutters about 1½ to 2 inches in diameter. Brush the tops of the scones with a little milk.

5.   Heat an ungreased baking sheet in the oven until it is warm. Place the scones on the sheet and bake near the top of the oven until they are a light golden brown, about 10 minutes.

6.   Remove the scones from the baking sheet and let them cool on a wire rack.

TO MAKE THE GLAZE:

In a small saucepan, combine the jelly, tarragon, and lemon juice. Heat gently over medium-low heat, stirring until melted. Let the glaze cool to room temperature.

TO MAKE THE FILLING:

Split the scones and butter both halves. Lay slices of turkey on the bottom half of each scone. Spread the turkey with glaze. Replace the tops of the scones and serve.

S P R E A D S

Ginger-Flavored Honey

Once the spice trade began between Europe and the Orient, ginger was one of the most prized foods and found its way into the cooking of England and eventually to America. It remains popular today on both sides of the Atlantic. We particularly enjoy the spicy flavor of ginger combined with the soft sweetness of the honey. If the candied ginger is too sticky to chop easily, chill it a bit first.

YIELD: 2 cups

2 cups (16 ounces) light-colored honey
¼ cup chopped candied ginger

In a small saucepan, stir the honey over medium heat until warmed through. Stir in the ginger. Pour the honey into a heat-proof jar and cover. Let the mixture cool to room temperature before serving.

Herb-Flavored Honey

This lightly scented honey is a fine addition to the tea tray and tastes very good indeed with Lemon Bread (page 57) or Sage Bread (page 56). It looks jewel-like served in cut glass or even an everyday glass jar. It may look like ordinary honey, but will not taste like it.

YIELD: 2 cups

2 cups (16 ounces) light-colored honey
6 to 7 sprigs fresh herb such as lavender, mint, thyme, or rosemary

In a small saucepan, stir the honey over medium heat until warmed through. Put the herb sprigs or the chopped leaves of the herb in a heat-proof jar and pour the honey over them. Cool to room temperature. Cover tightly and let the honey stand for a day or two before serving.

Herb-Flavored Honey

Orange Honey

Honey infused with fragrant orange zest is delicious with full-flavored breads. For the best results, select a robust honey such as clover or alfalfa, rather than a more delicate sort such as raspberry or blueberry. Pale golden specialty honeys, made by bees pollinating raspberry and blueberry bushes, taste light and delicious but they are not as full-bodied as clover or alfalfa honey.

YIELD: 1 cup

1 cup (8 ounces) honey
Grated zest of 1 orange

In a small saucepan, stir the honey over medium heat until warmed through. Stir in the orange zest. Pour the honey into a heat-proof jar and cover. Let the mixture cool before serving.

Berry-Flavored Honey

Heady with the essense of sweet summer berries, this honey is sublime when served with breads, scones, or muffins. Prepare it in the warm months when the berries are in season, to savour in the cold of winter.

YIELD: 2½ cups

2 cups (16 ounces) light-colored honey
½ cup fresh raspberries or strawberries

In a small saucepan, stir the honey over medium heat until warmed through. Add the berries and stir gently. Pour the mixture into a heat-proof jar and cool to room temperature. Cover tightly and let the honey stand at room temperature for 3 days, then refrigerate.

Compound Herb Butter

Compound butters are well-spiced spreads generally made several days before serving so the flavors have time to mingle. Try one on thinly sliced white bread or an herb-flavored bread. It is also delicious on a delicate tea sandwich made with ham, turkey, or chicken.

YIELD: 1 cup

¼ cup lightly packed fresh basil, parsley, or
* cilantro leaves*
1 medium scallion, white part only, chopped
½ cup (1 stick) cold butter, cut into pieces
1 teaspoon freshly squeezed lemon juice
¼ teaspoon dry mustard
¼ teaspoon freshly ground white pepper
¼ teaspoon salt
Few drops of bottled hot pepper sauce

1. In a food processor, combine the herbs and scallion. Process with on/off turns until both are finely chopped. Add the rest of the ingredients and process until the mixture is fluffy, scraping the sides often.
2. Scrape the butter onto a work surface and, with dry, cool hands, fashion it into a roll. Wrap the roll in plastic wrap and refrigerate for up to 1 week. For longer storage, wrap aluminum foil around the plastic and freeze the butter for a month or so.
3. Let the refrigerated butter stand at room temperature for 15 to 20 minutes before using and, if frozen, for 2 hours.

Sage Cheese Butter

Sage is a strong-flavored herb, so do resist temptation to add more than recommended. This butter is wonderful on rustic, just-baked peasant loaves. Here, we mix it with Parmesan and a little chopped parsley.

YIELD: 1 cup

½ cup (1 stick) butter, softened

2 tablespoons grated Parmesan cheese

2 tablespoons chopped fresh sage, or 1 teaspoon dried rubbed sage

1 tablespoon chopped fresh parsley, or 1 teaspoon dried parsley flakes

1. In a small bowl, beat the ingredients with an electric mixer set at medium speed until they are light and fluffy.

2. Cover the bowl and let the butter stand for 3 to 3½ hours to give the flavors time to blend.

3. Refrigerate, well-covered, for up to 3 days if you have used fresh herbs, and for 1 week or so if you have used dried herbs.

Tarragon-Mustard Butter

The mustard seed lends a zesty flavor to this butter. It's particularly good with thin slices of baked ham and a few sprigs of watercress tucked between whole-wheat or white bread.

YIELD: ½ cup

½ cup (1 stick) butter, softened

2 tablespoons chopped fresh tarragon, or 2 teaspoons dried tarragon leaves

½ teaspoon mustard seed, crushed

1. In a small bowl, beat all the ingredients with an electric mixer set at medium speed until they are light and fluffy.

2. Cover the bowl and let the butter stand at room temperature for 3 to 3½ hours to give the flavors time to blend.

3. Refrigerate the butter well-covered, for up to 3 days if you have used fresh tarragon, and for 1 week or so if you have used dried tarragon.

Strawberry Butter

Fresh creamery butter and luscious, ripe strawberries epitomize the grandeur of nature's bounty. Combining the two elevates them even further.

YIELD: 1 cup

½ cup (1 stick) butter, softened

¼ cup fresh strawberries, washed and hulled

2 to 3 tablespoons confectioners' sugar

Cut the butter into 6 to 8 pieces and put it in a food processor with the strawberries. Process the butter and strawberries, adding the confectioners' sugar while doing so, until the butter is smooth and even-colored. (To mix by hand, cream the butter and sugar, then mash the strawberries with a fork and mix them with the butter mixture.)

Blackberry Syrup

As with Spiced Blackberry Jam, fresh black-berries are best here, but cultivated boysenber-ries or frozen berries also work well. Prepared with raspberries, the syrup is so deep red it reminds one of liquid garnets.

YIELD: 2 cups of syrup with pulp,
          or 1 cup strained

3 cups fresh blackberries
¾ cup sugar
1½ teaspoons grated lemon zest
⅓ cup water

1.   In a heavy 3-quart saucepan, combine all the ingredients and mix gently. Cook over medium heat, stirring constantly, until the sugar dissolves.
2.   Bring the syrup to a boil over medium-high heat. Reduce the heat and simmer, uncovered, for about 8 minutes, stirring occasionally, until the fruit is soft.
3.   Cook for another 2 to 3 minutes and gently mash the berries against the side of pan with the back of a wooden spoon.

Spiced Blackberry Jam

4.   Cool the syrup to lukewarm. If desired, strain the fruit from the syrup by pressing the syrup through a sieve. Pour into a jar. Cover and refrigerate for up to 2 weeks.

Spiced Blackberry Jam

If you can, make this piquant jam with the wild, fresh blackberries that grow along coun-try roads. If you have no access to wild berries, choose the boysenberries or blackberries avail-able at farmers' markets. However, a craving for the sweet, cinnamon-touched jam should not go unanswered: The jam is delicious made with frozen berries, too.

YIELD: 1 quart

1 quart fresh blackberries, or frozen loose-pack
  unsweetened blackberries, thawed
¼ cup freshly squeezed lemon juice
4½ cups sugar
1½ teaspoons finely grated lemon zest
¼ teaspoon ground cinnamon
Cinnamon sticks

1.   In a heavy 4-quart saucepan, combine the berries and lemon juice. Bring to a boil over medium-high heat, stirring often.
2.   Stir in the sugar, lemon zest, and cin-namon, and let the mixture boil to dissolve the sugar.
3.   Reduce the heat to medium and boil gently for about 15 minutes, stirring often, until the temperature reaches 220°F on a candy thermometer. (Subtract 2°F for each 1,000 feet above sea level.)
4.   Remove the pot from the heat. Stir the jam with a long-handled spoon and skim off any foam that rises to the top.

5. Ladle the jam into hot, sterilized half-pint canning jars, leaving a ¼-inch space on top. Place a piece of cinnamon stick in the jam in each jar. Seal with canning lids according to manufacturer's directions.

6. Cool the jars upright on a wire rack. Store in the refrigerator up to 1 month. For longer storage, process the jars in a boiling-water bath for 5 minutes after sealing. (Add an additional minute of processing time for each 1,000 feet above sea level.) Cool on a rack and label. Store the jars in a cool, dry, and dark place.

Old-Fashioned Sauces for Puddings

There was a time when a pudding was not considered complete without a satiny sauce to accompany it. These three can be served with the puddings found in this book. Try the Hazelnut Sauce with the Feathery Chocolate Pudding (page 85) and the Lemon Sauce or Rose Sauce with the Country French Prune Pudding (page 87).

YIELD: About 1½ cups

Sauce Base:
½ *cup sugar*
1 *tablespoon cornstarch*
1 *cup boiling water*
1 *tablespoon butter, flaked*

1. In a small saucepan, combine the sugar and cornstarch. Add the boiling water and whisk until smooth.

2. Over medium-high heat, continue whisking the sugar mixture until it boils and thickens.

3. Reduce the heat to medium-low and cook for 5 minutes, whisking occasionally.

A Breakfast Tea

Raised Waffles

Lemon Thyme Bread

Pumpkin Nut Bread

Heavenly Hots

Blackberry Syrup

Strawberry Butter

Orange Honey

Mint Tea

4. Add the butter, a few flakes at a time, whisking well after each addition until each flake is incorporated.

Rose Sauce:
2 *tablespoons red currant jelly*
½ *to 1 teaspoon rose water*

Add the jelly to the hot base and whisk until melted. Whisk in the rose water. Serve the sauce warm.

Lemon Sauce:
Juice and zest of 1 lemon
½ *teaspoon ground nutmeg*

Add the lemon juice, lemon zest, and nutmeg to the hot base. Whisk until blended. Serve the sauce warm.

Hazelnut Sauce:
¼ *cup Frangelico liqueur*
¼ *cup chopped hazelnuts*
½ *teaspoon ground cinnamon*

Add the liqueur, hazelnuts, and cinnamon to the hot base. Whisk until blended. Serve the sauce warm.

COOKIES

Grilled Marmalade Fingers

The essence of an authentic tea, marmalade fingers are easy and tasty. The queen in the nursery rhyme may have preferred butter to marmalade for her bread, but with these dainty fingers you can enjoy both.

YIELD: 18 fingers

6 slices whole-wheat bread
5 to 6 teaspoons butter, softened
4 to 6 tablespoons orange marmalade
½ cup coarsely chopped pecans

1.   Preheat the boiler. Toast the bread slices lightly.
2.   Spread each slice sparingly with butter, then spread each with 2 to 3 teaspoons of marmalade, being sure the marmalade goes all the way to the edges. Sprinkle the chopped pecans evenly over the marmalade-covered bread slices.
3.   Arrange the toasts on a baking sheet, marmalade side up, and place them under the broiler for 1 to 2 minutes, or until the marmalade begins to bubble and pecans are lightly toasted. The bread crusts may be slightly charred.
4.   Carefully cut off the charred crusts and then cut each slice into 3 strips, or "fingers." Handle the toast carefully as the marmalade will be very hot. Serve the marmalade fingers immediately.

Jam Cookies

Jam-filled cookies are fun to make. Pair them with Dream Cookies (page 71) and Meringue Kisses (page 75), and they'll be consumed in the time they took to bake.

YIELD: 3½ to 4 dozen cookies

1 cup (2 sticks) butter, softened
½ cup sugar
1 egg yolk
½ teaspoon almond or vanilla extract
2½ cups all-purpose flour
⅓ cup raspberry and/or apricot jam

1.   In the medium bowl of an electric mixer, beat the butter and sugar at medium speed until they are light and fluffy. Beat in the egg yolk and extract. With the mixer at low speed, gradually beat in the flour until well blended. Cover and refrigerate for at least 2 hours.
2.   Preheat the oven to 350°F. Roll the chilled dough into 1-inch balls. Place them 2 inches apart on unbuttered baking sheets.
3.   Indent the centers of each ball slightly with your thumb. Then place a rounded ¼-teaspoon measuring spoon of the jam into each depression. Pinch together any split edges on the cookies to hold in the jam.
4.   Bake the cookies for 15 minutes or until they are golden. Cool on wire racks and serve.

Raspberry and Lemon Curd Hearts

These little heart-shaped sandwiches, with dark red raspberry jam or bright lemon curd peeking through them, are festive on the tea table. Make them with very firm slices of thin white bread from the bakery. If you use cookie cutters that measure differently from the ones we call for, be sure the bread is large enough to accommodate them.

YIELD: 12 heart sandwiches

24 slices thin white bread, each 3 inches wide
¼ cup raspberry jam
¼ cup lemon curd

1. Cut a heart shape from each of the 24 slices of bread using a 2⅝-inch heart-shaped cookie cutter. In 12 of the heart-shaped pieces, use a 2-inch or smaller heart-shaped cookie cutter to make heart cutouts in the center of each. Discard the small heart pieces.
2. Spread 6 whole hearts with about 2 teaspoons of raspberry jam each. Spread the remaining 6 whole hearts with about 2 tea-spoons of lemon curd each. Top each with a cutout heart.
3. Carefully place the sandwiches on the rack of a toaster oven and toast as you would ordinarily, until the bread is a light, golden brown. Serve immediately.

    Note: If you do not have a toaster oven, toast the bread hearts before spreading with jam for 10 to 20 seconds under a preheated broiler. Turn them and toast the other sides for a few seconds, or until they are a light golden brown. Spread the whole hearts with jam or curd, as described above, and assemble. Serve immediately.

Dream Cookies

Light and crisp and buttery, Dream Cookies are ever so easy to eat. The batter is simple to mix, and since it must chill for at least an hour, these cookies are a good choice when you are planning ahead.

YIELD: 4 dozen cookies

2 cups all-purpose flour
1 teaspoon baking powder
1 cup (2 sticks) butter, softened
¾ cup sugar
2 teaspoons vanilla extract
24 blanched whole almonds, halved lengthwise

1. In a medium bowl, sift together the flour and baking powder. Set aside.
2. In the medium bowl of an electric mixer, beat the butter, sugar, and vanilla at medium speed until the mixture is light and fluffy, scraping the sides of the bowl often. Add the dry ingredients to the creamed mixture until it is blended and smooth. Cover the dough with plastic wrap and refrigerate for 1 hour.
3. Preheat the oven to 300°F. Roll the chilled dough into 1-inch balls. Place them 2½ inches apart on unbuttered baking sheets. Gently press an almond half in the top of each ball.
4. Bake the cookies for 25 minutes, or until they turn a very pale golden color. The cookies will be very light and crisp. Cool them on wire racks. Serve the cookies or store them in an airtight container.

Madeleines

Of all the cakes, cookies, and sandwiches that are passed as tea is poured, none equals the perfection of a fragrant, tenderly warm madeleine. The cookie has a delicate crumb and a fragile flavor that gently echoes a few drops of fresh lemon.

YIELD: 2 dozen cookies

⅔ cup superfine sugar
3 eggs
1 egg yolk
Juice of ½ lemon
Pinch of salt
1¼ cups all-purpose flour, sifted
½ cup (1 stick) butter, melted

1. Preheat the oven to 350°F and butter 24 madeleine molds.
2. In the medium bowl of an electric mixer, beat the sugar, whole eggs, egg yolk, lemon juice, and salt at low speed until they are well blended. Fold in the flour until it is well combined. Slowly add the melted butter to the mixture, and stir to blend.
3. Spoon the batter into the molds, filling them no more than ⅔ full.
4. Bake the cookies for 20 to 25 minutes, or until they are slightly golden. Unmold and cool the cookies on wire racks and serve.

Lime Wafers

Crisp, thin, and light, these sprightly lime-flavored wafers are spiced with just a wisp of ginger. For nice thin wafers, roll only in one direction, beginning at the middle and working outward.

YIELD: About 4 dozen wafers

1 cup (2 sticks) butter, softened
2 cups sugar
3 eggs
1 teaspoon grated lime zest
3 tablespoons freshly squeezed lime juice
½ teaspoon salt
¼ teaspoon ground ginger
5 cups all-purpose flour, sifted

1. In the large bowl of an electric mixer, cream the butter for 2 to 3 minutes at medium speed until it is light. Gradually add the sugar, beating for 2 to 3 minutes, until the mixture is light and fluffy. Scrape the sides of the bowl often. Add the eggs, lime zest, lime juice, salt, and ginger. Beat well. With the mixer at low speed, gradually beat in the flour until well blended.
2. Divide the dough into 4 equal pieces. Wrap each piece in plastic and refrigerate for at least 2 hours.
3. Preheat the oven to 375°F. Butter 2 baking sheets.
4. On a well-floured work surface, roll 1

Lime Wafers

piece of chilled dough into an 8½-inch-diameter circle about ¼-inch thick. Keep the remaining dough refrigerated until you are ready to roll it.

5.   When a piece of the dough is rolled, cut out the wafers with a 2-inch round cookie cutter or an upturned glass. Using a floured metal spatula, lift the cookies and arrange them 1 inch apart on the baking sheets. Repeat with the remaining dough.

6.   Bake the cookies for 15 to 17 minutes, or until the edges of the wafers are lightly browned. Cool the wafers on wire racks. Serve the cookies or store them in an air-tight container.

Black Walnut Linzer Hearts

These little jam-filled black walnut cookies are the jewels of the tea table. However, since black walnuts are a little difficult to find, you may prefer to use English walnuts.

YIELD: 1 dozen cookies

1 cup (2 sticks) butter, softened
½ cup granulated sugar
2 cups all-purpose flour
⅓ cup ground black or English walnuts
½ teaspoon salt
1 to 2 tablespoons raspberry or blackberry jam
Confectioners' sugar

1.   In the medium bowl of an electric mixer, cream the butter and granulated sugar at high speed until light and fluffy. Add the flour, walnuts, and salt. Stir until the mixture forms a soft dough; wrap in plastic and refrigerate for 45 minutes.

2.   Preheat the oven to 375°F. Butter 2 baking sheets.

A Bridal Shower Tea

Stilton, Pear, and Watercress Savory

Sage Bread

Sage Cheese Butter

Tarragon-Mustard Butter

Blackberry Tarts

Raspberry and Lemon Curd Hearts

Black Walnut Linzer Hearts

Chocolate Walnut Torte

Lovers' Tea

White Winter Champagne Punch

---

3.   On a floured work surface, roll the chilled dough into a circle about ¼-inch thick. Cut into heart shapes using a 2⅝-inch heart-shaped cookie cutter. Using a 2-inch or smaller heart-shaped cookie cutter, cut out the centers of half of the hearts. Carefully place the cookies on the baking sheets about 1 inch apart.

4.   Bake for 12 to 14 minutes, or until the cookies are lightly browned. Cool the cookies on wire racks.

5.   Spread each whole heart cookie with ½ to 1 teaspoon of jam, leaving a border around the edge. Sift confectioners' sugar on the cookies with the cut-out hearts. Place these, sugar side up, on the jam-topped cookies. Serve the cookies immediately or store in an airtight container.

Gingerbread Girls and Boys

Big and chewy, these gingerbread cookies are loved by children, as well as the child in all of us. Make them for a nursery tea or during the holiday season for pure fun and yummy taste. Besides the familiar gingerbread man cutter, girl and boy versions can be found at specialty bake stores. When you are decorating the cookies, you may want to cut the raisins in two to make eyes and buttons.

YIELD: 3 dozen cookies

5 cups all-purpose flour
1½ teaspoons baking soda
1 tablespoon ground ginger
2 teaspoons dried ground lemon zest
1 teaspoon ground cinnamon
½ teaspoon ground cloves
⅓ teaspoon ground nutmeg
1 cup (2 sticks) butter, softened
1 cup sugar
1 egg
1 cup molasses
2 tablespoons freshly squeezed lemon juice
Raisins, for decoration

1. In a medium bowl, stir together the flour, baking soda, ginger, lemon zest, cinnamon, cloves, and nutmeg. Set aside.
2. In the medium bowl of an electric mixer, cream the butter and sugar at medium speed for about 5 minutes, until the mixture is fluffy, scraping the sides of the bowl often. Add the egg, molasses, and lemon juice to the mixture. Beat until blended. Gradually add the dry ingredients into the egg mixture with the mixer set at low speed until blended.
3. Divide the dough into 4 equal pieces.

Wrap each piece in plastic and refrigerate for at least 3 hours.
4. Preheat the oven to 375°F. Butter 2 baking sheets and line them with parchment or wax paper. Lightly butter the paper.
5. On a well-floured work surface, roll 1 piece of chilled dough into a circle about ⅛-inch thick. Keep the remaining dough refrigerated until you are ready to roll it.
6. When a piece of the dough is rolled, flour a 4-inch gingerbread cookie cutter and cut out as many cookies as possible from it. Gather together the scraps, reroll them and cut out more cookies. Using a floured metal spatula, gently lift the cookies and put them 1 inch apart on the baking sheets. Decorate with raisin buttons down their fronts and with raisins for eyes. Repeat with the remaining pieces of dough.
7. Bake the cookies for 6 to 7 minutes, or until they are puffed and set.
8. Cool the cookies on the baking sheets for 1 minute and then transfer them to wire racks to cool completely. Serve the cookies or store in an airtight container.

Jam Cookies (page 70), Dream Cookies (page 71) and Meringue Kisses

Rose Water Sugar Cookies

These big, crisp sugar cookies are sweet and subtly scented with rose water.

YIELD: 5 dozen cookies

4½ cups all-purpose flour, sifted
1 teaspoon baking powder
1 teaspoon baking soda
1 teaspoon salt
1 cup (2 sticks) butter, softened
1½ cups sugar
2 eggs
1 cup sour cream
1 tablespoon rose water
Sugar

1. In a medium bowl, sift together the flour, baking powder, baking soda, and salt.
2. In the large bowl of an electric mixer, cream the butter and sugar at medium speed for 4 to 5 minutes until it is light and fluffy, scraping down the side of the bowl often. Add the eggs, one at a time, beating well after each addition. With the mixer at low speed add the dry ingredients to the egg mixture, alternating with the sour cream and rose water. Beat well.
3. Divide the dough into 3 pieces and wrap each in plastic. Refrigerate for at least 4 hours or overnight.
4. Preheat the oven to 375°F. On a well-floured surface, roll each piece of the chilled dough into a circle about ¼-inch thick. Cut the cookies with floured 3-inch cookie cutters.
5. Using a floured metal spatula, arrange the cookies 1 inch apart on unbuttered baking sheets. Sprinkle the cookies with sugar and bake for 12 minutes, or until they are lightly browned. Cool on racks and serve.

Meringue Kisses

Just airy swirls of sweet flavor, Meringue Kisses are so easy to make. But it is not a good idea to make meringues on a humid day, as they will never harden to the right consistency: crispy outside, a little chewy within.

YIELD: 5 dozen kisses

4 egg whites, at room temperature
⅛ teaspoon cream of tartar
1 cup sugar

1. Preheat the oven to 225°F and butter 2 baking sheets. Line each baking sheet with parchment or wax paper and butter well.
2. In the small bowl of an electric mixer, beat the egg whites at high speed until they are frothy. Add the cream of tartar. Continue beating at high speed and add the sugar, 1 tablespoon at a time, beating for 30 seconds after each addition for the first ½ cup. For the second ½ cup, beat the meringue for 10 to 15 seconds after each tablespoon of sugar. Total beating time will be about 10 minutes, at which point the meringue should be stiff, smooth, and glossy.
3. Spoon the meringue into a large pastry bag fitted with a large star tip. Pipe swirled, peaked "kiss" shapes onto the baking sheets, leaving about 1 inch between each.
4. Bake the meringues for 60 minutes, or until they are slightly golden. Turn the oven off, but do not open the door. Let the meringue kisses stand in the turned-off oven for 1 hour. Serve right away, or store in an airtight container.

CAKES

Lemon Ginger Pound Cake

Lemon and fresh ginger are a perfect marriage, and nowhere is their compatibility more apparent than in this buttery pound cake glazed with sweetened lemon juice.

YIELD: 16 servings

3 cups all-purpose flour
2 teaspoons baking powder
½ teaspoon salt
1 cup (2 sticks) butter, softened
2 cups sugar
4 eggs
1 cup milk
Grated zest of 2 lemons
2 teaspoons grated fresh ginger
¼ cup sugar, for glaze
3 tablespoons freshly squeezed lemon juice, for glaze

1. Preheat the oven to 350°F. Butter and flour four 7 ½ x 3½ x 2-inch loaf pans, or two 9 x 5 x 3-inch loaf pans. Shake out any excess flour.
2. In a medium bowl, sift together the flour, baking powder, and salt. Set aside.
3. In the large bowl of an electric mixer, cream the butter and sugar at medium speed until they are fluffy, scraping the sides of the bowl often. Add the eggs one at a time, beating well after each addition. Add the flour mixture to the batter, alter-nating it with the milk and beating at low speed until blended. Fold in the lemon zest and ginger. Divide the batter evenly among the prepared pans.
4. Bake for 45 to 50 minutes for small loaves or 60 to 65 minutes for large loaves, or until a toothpick inserted into the center of a cake comes out clean.
5. Cool the cakes still in the pans for 10 minutes on wire racks. While the cakes are cooling in the pans, combine the sugar and lemon juice in a small bowl and mix well.
6. Remove the cakes from the pans and set them on the racks placed over sheet pans or foil. Brush the lemon glaze on the cakes while they are still hot.

Hickory Nut Butter Cakes

Hickory Nut Butter Cakes

The glaze for these little treasures is similar to the one for the Ambrosia Torte (page 81), but the cake, chock-full of buttery hickory nuts, tastes quite unique. The fluted cakes look elegant set on a large doily-lined pedestal cake stand or mixed with an assortment of cookies and slices of dessert bread.

YIELD: 12 servings

3 cups all-purpose flour
2 teaspoons baking powder
1 cup (2 sticks) butter, softened
2 cups granulated sugar
Grated zest from 1 orange
3 eggs
1 cup milk
1 teaspoon vanilla extract
1 cup chopped hickory nuts, pecans, or walnuts

Orange Glaze:
1 cup confectioners' sugar
¼ teaspoon vanilla extract
4 to 6 teaspoons orange juice

TO MAKE THE CAKES:

1. Preheat oven to 350°F. Spray twelve 1-cup fluted mini-tube pan cups with non-stick coating spray.
2. In a medium bowl, combine the flour and baking powder. Stir a few times to mix well. Set aside.
3. In the large bowl of an electric mixer, cream the butter and sugar at medium speed for about 5 minutes, or until they are light and fluffy, scraping the sides of the bowl often. Add the orange zest and the eggs, one at a time, beating well after each addition. Add the dry ingredients to the egg mixture, alternating it with the milk. With the mixer at low speed, blend the ingre-

dients after each addition. When all the flour and milk are incorporated into the batter, add the vanilla and mix well. Fold in the nuts. Spread the batter evenly in the prepared cups, using about ⅔ cup of batter for each.
4. Bake for 20 to 25 minutes, or until a toothpick inserted in the center of a cake comes out clean.
5. Set the pans on wire racks and let the cakes cool for 15 minutes. Run a knife carefully around the edges of the cakes to loosen them. Remove the cakes from the pans and cool completely on the racks.

TO MAKE THE GLAZE:

In a small bowl, combine the confectioners' sugar, vanilla, and enough orange juice to achieve a thin consistency. Drizzle the glaze over the cooled cakes.

A Garden Tea

Spinach Cheese Tartlets
Blackberry Muffin Miniatures
Spiced Blackberry Jam
Hickory Nut Butter Cakes
Country Peach and Plum Tart
Marmalade Torte Paradiso
Iced Clove Cooler
Orange-Clove Tea
Lemon-Mint Tea

Blackberry Jam Cake

The familiar flavor of lemonade lightly permeates this simple cream-frosted cake. Inside, deep, dark, sweet blackberry jam provides a delightful contrast of taste, texture, and color. As if by decree, the cake is festooned with the season's first pansies for true high summer tea.

YIELD: 12 servings

2¼ cups cake flour
1¼ cups granulated sugar
2 teaspoons baking powder
¼ teaspoon salt
¼ cup frozen lemonade concentrate, thawed
1¼ cups heavy cream, chilled
3 eggs
½ teaspoon vanilla extract

Frosting:
1½ cups heavy cream, chilled
2 tablespoons confectioners' sugar
2 tablespoons frozen lemonade concentrate, thawed

Filling and Garnish:
¾ cup blackberry jam or preserves
Purple pansies and fresh blackberries

TO MAKE THE CAKE:

1.   Preheat the oven to 350°F. Butter and flour two 8-inch round cake pans. Shake out any excess flour.

2.   In a small bowl, stir together the flour, sugar, baking powder, and salt. Set aside.

3.   In a chilled small mixing bowl of an electric mixer, gradually beat the lemonade concentrate into the cream at low speed. Increase the speed to medium and beat until the mixture holds its shape. Transfer the mixture to a large bowl and set aside.

4.   In another small bowl of an electric mixer beat the eggs and vanilla with clean beaters set at high speed until the mixture is thick and lemon colored, about 5 minutes. Fold the egg mixture into the cream mixture. Then gently fold in the dry ingredients. When evenly mixed, divide the batter equally between the prepared pans.

5.   Bake the cake for 30 to 35 minutes, or until a toothpick inserted in the center comes out clean.

6.   Cool the cakes in the pans on wire racks for 10 minutes; then remove the layers and let them cool completely on the racks.

TO MAKE THE FROSTING:

In a chilled bowl of an electric mixer, combine the cream and confectioners' sugar. With the mixer set at low speed, gradually beat in the lemonade concentrate. Increase the speed to medium and beat until stiff peaks form.

TO ASSEMBLE THE CAKE:

Arrange one cake layer on a serving plate and spread it with jam or preserves. Place the other layer on top. Cover the top and sides of the cake with the frosting and refrigerate for at least 2 hours. Decorate with pansies and blackberries.

Blackberry Jam Cake

Chocolate Walnut Torte

Use your favorite pie crust recipe or the pastry from Honey Tart (page 82) for this sumptuous chocolate and nut extravaganza.

When caramelizing the sugar for the filling, be sure to use a heavy saucepan. If the pan is too thin, the sugar will burn. Stir the sugar 3 or 4 times a minute at the beginning of the cooking; once the sugar begins to stick together and form tiny clumps, it is crucial to stir it constantly. Use a sturdy wooden spoon with a long handle or a metal spoon with an insulated handle and always protect your hands with potholders.

Be sure to take the pan from the heat before stirring in the cream. If you do not, the hot sugar may seize when the cream is added and form a hard mass in the bottom of the pan, which is virtually impossible to dissolve. When heating the cream and sugar, make sure the heat is turned down to medium-low; the moderate heat will prevent seizing while the last of the sugar crystals dissolve. Let the mixture cool gradually off the heat.

YIELD: 6 to 8 servings

Caramel Walnut Filling:

1 cup sugar

1 cup heavy cream, warmed

¼ cup light rum

3 tablespoons honey

About 2⅔ cups walnuts, chopped

Torte:

Pastry for a 2-crust, 9-inch pie

2 ounces semisweet chocolate, chopped

1 egg

1 tablespoon water

TO MAKE THE FILLING:

1.   In a heavy medium-size saucepan, heat the sugar over medium-low heat, stirring often, until the sugar starts to form small clumps. Continue to cook, stirring constantly, until the sugar turns golden but has not melted. This will take about 20 to 25 minutes. Remove the pan from the heat.

2.   Slowly stir in the warmed cream. The sugar will become lumpy. Return the pan to medium-low heat for about 5 minutes, and stir slowly to dissolve most of the sugar lumps. Remove the pan from the heat. Add the rum and honey and mix well. Stir in the walnuts.

TO ASSEMBLE THE TART:

1.   Preheat the oven to 350°F. Butter a 9-inch tart pan with a removable bottom.

2.   On a lightly floured work surface, roll out two-thirds of the pastry into a 9-inch circle. Line the prepared tart pan with the pastry, pressing it into the bottom and sides of the pan. Set the tart pan on a baking sheet and sprinkle the chopped chocolate over the bottom of the pastry shell. Pour the caramel-nut filling over the chocolate.

3.   Roll out the remaining pastry on a lightly floured work surface. Cut the pastry into ½-inch strips. Weave the strips diagonally to form a lattice top on the tart. Crimp the edges of the tart.

4.   In a small bowl, beat together the egg and water with a fork. Brush the pastry with the egg wash.

5.   Bake for 50 minutes, or until the filling is bubbling and the crust is golden brown. Cool the tart in the pan on a wire rack.

Lily of the Valley Cake

When selecting a filling for this traditional butter cake, choose one that complements the flavoring in the buttercream. For instance, if you decide to flavor the buttercream with Framboise, spread strawberry or raspberry preserves between the cake layers. If you choose to omit the liqueur and use only lemon zest, you may decide to fill the cake with lemon curd.

YIELD: 10 to 12 servings

6 eggs, at room temperature
1 cup sugar
2 teaspoons finely grated lemon zest
1½ cups all-purpose flour
¼ cup (½ stick) butter, melted

French Buttercream:
1⅔ cups sugar
½ cup water
6 egg whites, at room temperature
¼ teaspoon cream of tartar
Pinch of salt
2½ cups (5 sticks) butter, softened
2 teaspoons finely grated lemon zest, optional
2 teaspoons liqueur such as Grand Marnier,
   Kahlúa, Framboise, or your favorite, optional

Filling:
About ½ cup fruit preserves or jam or lemon curd

TO MAKE THE CAKE:

1.   Preheat the oven to 350°F. Butter and flour two 8-inch round cake pans. Line the bottom of each pan with wax paper. Butter and flour the wax paper and the sides of the pans. Shake out any excess flour.
2.   In a medium saucepan, whisk the eggs with the sugar and lemon zest until they are blended. Set the pan over low heat and whisk until the mixture is warm.
3.   Pour the mixture into a large bowl of a electric mixer and beat at high speed for about 7 minutes, or until the batter is light and fluffy.
4.   Slowly sift the flour over the batter and gently fold it in. Do not overmix. Gradually fold in the melted butter, folding just until the batter is smooth. Fill the prepared pans with equal amounts of batter. Tap them gently on the counter to release air bubbles.
5.   Bake the cakes with the pans set on a baking sheet for 28 to 30 minutes, or until the cake is golden and springs back when gently touched in the center.
6.   Cool the cakes still in the pans on wire racks for 5 minutes. Invert the cakes onto the racks and peel off the paper. Allow them to cool thoroughly.

TO MAKE THE BUTTERCREAM:

1.   Combine the sugar and water in a large, heavy saucepan. Slowly stir to dissolve some of the sugar.
2.   Cook the mixture over high heat, without stirring, until it is boiling. Cover the pan, reduce the heat to medium high, and boil for 5 minutes.
3.   Remove the lid and let the syrup boil until it reaches 242°F on a candy thermometer.
4.   Meanwhile, in the medium bowl of an electric mixer, beat the egg whites, cream of tartar, and salt at high speed until stiff peaks form.
5.   As soon as the syrup reaches the desired temperature, add it in droplets to the beaten egg whites, continuing to beat them at high speed. When a third of the syrup is incorporated, add the rest in a slow, steady stream while still beating at high speed.

Beat the meringue until it cools, about 10 to 12 minutes.

6. While beating the meringue, cream the softened butter in a medium bowl, using another electric mixer or a hand-held mixer, until it is light and fluffy. If you have only one mixer, cream the butter before you begin making the meringue and hold it at room temperature.

7. Once the meringue is cool, beat in the butter, a dessert-spoonful at a time. (If the meringue is not cool, the butter will melt.) Add the lemon zest and the liqueur. Beat briefly to incorporate.

TO ASSEMBLE THE CAKE:

1. Brush the crumbs off the cake and, if necessary, even the layers with a knife.

2. Place the bottom layer on a serving plate. Spread it with fruit preserves, jam, or lemon curd.

3. Position the second layer on the filling. Frost the sides and top of the cake with a thin layer of buttercream. Refrigerate the cake for 10 to 15 minutes or until the buttercream is chilled. Frost the cake with a second, more luxuriant coat of buttercream.

4. Serve the cake at once or refrigerate it for later serving. Because of the amount of butter in the frosting, the cake cannot sit at room temperature very long. Take it from the refrigerator about 30 minutes before serving to take off the chill.

Ambrosia Torte

This torte takes only minutes to put together and a mere half hour to bake. Another reason to select the torte is its delectable flavor, highlighted by the simple glaze adorned with candied zest and almonds.

YIELD: 6 to 8 servings

⅔ cup all-purpose flour
½ teaspoon baking powder
⅔ cup (1⅓ sticks) butter, softened
⅔ cup granulated sugar
2 eggs
1 teaspoon almond extract, optional

Glaze and Garnish:
1 tablespoon orange juice
⅓ cup confectioners' sugar
About ¾ cup chopped candied orange zest and chopped almonds
Orange sections, thinly sliced

TO MAKE THE TORTE:

1. Preheat the oven to 350°F. Butter and flour an 8-inch round cake pan. Shake out any excess flour.

2. In a small bowl, sift together the flour and baking powder. Set aside.

3. In the medium bowl of an electric mixer, beat the butter and sugar at medium speed until they are creamy and fluffy, scraping the sides of the bowl often. Add the eggs and almond extract. Beat for about 2 minutes, until light and smooth. Add the dry ingredients to the creamed batter and stir thoroughly until blended. Spread the batter in the prepared pan.

4. Bake for 30 minutes, or until the top of the torte springs back when touched

(continued)

lightly near the center.

5.   Cool the torte in the pan on a wire rack for 10 minutes. Remove the torte from the pan and allow it to cool completely on the rack. If the torte sags slightly in the center as it cools, invert it to serve.

TO MAKE THE GLAZE:

Gradually stir the orange juice into the confectioners' sugar until smooth. Spread the glaze evenly over the top of the torte and sprinkle with the chopped candied orange zest, almonds, and a pinwheel of thinly sliced orange sections.

Honey Tart

Tender crust and pretty lattice work make this rich tart, baked with a honey-kissed cheese filling, especially appealing. When weaving a lattice top, be sure the work surface is well floured to prevent the strips from sticking and tearing when you lift them up to arrange on the tart. Lay them gently on the filling, doing so at an angle from your vantage point. This will help you keep the strips looking even and straight. And finally, avoid the temptation to press the strips into the filling or edges of the pastry to ensure that the lattice will bake without cracking.

YIELD: 8 servings

Cheese Filling:
1½ cups (12 ounces) cream cheese, softened
¾ cup (6 ounces) cottage cheese
⅓ cup honey, preferably orange blossom
3 tablespoons sour cream
3 tablespoons honey liqueur or orange liqueur
2 teaspoons grated orange zest

A Picnic Tea

Herbed Cream Cheese Sandwiches

Currant Scones with Smoked Turkey

Compound Herb Butter

Herb-Flavored Honey

Lime Wafers

Honey Tart

Lavender and Lime

Strawberry Tea

Pastry:
2 cups all-purpose flour
¼ cup sugar
Pinch of salt
10 tablespoons (1¼ sticks) butter, cut in pieces
1 tablespoon grated orange zest
2 egg yolks, beaten
2 tablespoons cold water

TO MAKE THE CHEESE FILLING:

In the small bowl of an electric mixer beat the cream cheese, cottage cheese, honey, sour cream, liqueur, and orange zest at medium speed until blended. Cover and refrigerate for 2 to 3 hours.

TO MAKE THE PASTRY:

1.   In the bowl of a food processor fitted with a metal blade, combine the flour, sugar, and salt. Distribute the butter and orange zest over the flour mixture. Process with on-off pulses until the mixture resembles fine meal.

2.   In a small mixing bowl, whisk together the egg yolks and cold water. With the processor running, gradually add the yolks to the other ingredients just until blended and cohesive. Do not mix so much that the dough forms a ball.

3.   Turn the dough out onto a lightly floured work surface and knead it with your fingertips until it forms a ball. Wrap the dough in plastic and refrigerate it for at least 30 minutes.

4.   Take the chilled dough from the refrigerator and divide it into 2 pieces, one containing about two-thirds of the dough, the other about a third. Rewrap the smaller piece and refrigerate it. Roll out the larger piece of dough on a floured work surface into a 12-inch square. Line a 10-inch square tart pan with the dough, pressing it into the bottoms and the sides. Trim the edges of the dough with a sharp knife. Place the tart pan on a baking sheet and freeze for 1 hour.

5.   Preheat the oven to 350°F. Prick the cold pastry all over with a fork. Line the pastry with a double thickness of foil and fill the foil with dried beans, rice, or pastry weights to keep the pastry flat during baking.

6.   Bake for 15 minutes, or until the pastry begins to brown around the edges. Remove the foil and weights. Prick the pastry again and continue baking for 5 to 10 minutes, or until it is golden.

7.   Cool the baked tart shell on a wire rack. Do not turn off the oven unless you do not plan to assemble and bake the tart for several hours.

TO ASSEMBLE THE TART:

1.   If you turned off the oven after making the pastry, preheat it to 350°F. Fill the

Honey Tart

cooled pastry shell with the cheese filling.

2.   On a floured work surface, roll the remaining piece of pastry into a 10-inch square. Cut into ½-inch wide strips. Arrange half the strips in rows on top of the tart. Lay the remaining strips at an angle over the first strips. Trim the ends of the pastry strips so that they are flush with the edge of tart. Do not attach the pastry strips to the baked crust.

3.   Bake the assembled tart set on a baking sheet for 40 to 50 minutes, or until the filling is set. Cool the tart on a wire rack.

A Mad Tea Party

"Take some more tea," the March Hare said to Alice, very earnestly.

"I've had nothing yet," Alice replied in an offended tone: "so I can't take more."

"You mean you can't take less," said the Hatter: "it's very easy to take more than nothing."

Lewis Carroll
ALICE IN WONDERLAND

Country Peach and Plum Tart

This free-form tart is summertime itself. The sweet, nutty layer of frangipane snuggled beneath the juicy plums and peaches adds an unexpected dimension of taste and texture, heightened by the crisp, fragile pastry. Traditionally, frangipane is made with eggs, sugar, and milk and flavored heavily with almond, or sometimes macaroons.

YIELD: 12 servings

Pastry:
2 cups all-purpose flour
2 teaspoons grated orange zest
1 teaspoon granulated sugar
½ teaspoon salt
½ teaspoon ground cloves
½ cup (1 stick) butter, cut into 8 pieces
1 egg yolk
⅓ cup cold water

Frangipane:
1 cup blanched slivered almonds
2 egg whites
¾ cup confectioners' sugar
½ teaspoon almond extract

Filling:
1 pound small dark plums, pitted and halved
  (7 or 8 plums)
¾ pound peaches, pitted and cut into eighths
  (about 3 peaches)
2 tablespoons granulated sugar
1 teaspoon ground cinnamon
2 tablespoons (¼ stick) butter

Glaze and Garnish:
1 tablespoon plum or orange liqueur
½ cup apricot jam
Fresh mint sprigs
Whipped cream

Country Peach and Plum Tart

TO MAKE THE PASTRY:

1.   In a large bowl, combine the flour, orange zest, sugar, salt, and cloves and mix well. Add the butter. Using a pastry blender or 2 kitchen knives, cut the butter into the mixture until it resembles coarse crumbs.
2.   Add the egg yolk and cold water. Mix the dough with your hands until it forms a moist ball. Wrap the pastry dough in plastic and refrigerate it for at least 45 minutes, or until you are ready to use it.

TO MAKE THE FRANGIPANE:

1.   In a food processor fitted with a metal blade, process the almonds until they are pulverized, about 1 minute.
2.   Add the egg whites, confectioners' sugar, and almond extract. Process until well blended and set aside.

TO MAKE THE FILLING:

1.   In a large bowl, combine the fruit.
2.   Mix the sugar and cinnamon together and add them to the fruit. Toss lightly with the fruit.

TO ASSEMBLE THE TART:

1.   Preheat the oven to 400°F. On a lightly floured work surface, roll the chilled dough into a 16 x 12-inch rectangle. Gently fold the dough into quarters. Lay the folded dough on an unbuttered baking sheet and unfold it. Spread the frangipane over the dough, leaving a 2-inch border on all sides. Arrange the fruit on top of the frangipane. Fold the dough's 2-inch border over the fruit to make an edge that will hold in the juices. Repair any cracks in the edge of the dough and pinch the corners together to seal. Dot the fruit with the butter.

2.   Bake for 50 to 60 minutes, or until the fruit is tender and the crust is golden.

3.   Cool the tart on a wire rack. Combine the liqueur and jam in a small saucepan and heat gently, stirring constantly, until the jam melts. Drizzle the apricot glaze over the fruit, add fresh mint sprigs, and serve with whipped cream.

Feathery Chocolate Pudding

For a light chocolate pudding with a soft, cake-like texture, try this at tea time. Steamed puddings have long been a tradition in the British Isles — particularly at Christmas time, when plum puddings are set on nearly every table — and as such seem an appropriate choice for tea. Our chocolate pudding, steamed a mere half hour, is light as a feather thanks to the whipped egg whites and the gentle art of steaming. Serve it with whipped cream, or with the Old-Fashioned Sauces for Puddings (page 69).

YIELD: 4 servings

1½ tablespoons butter
1 ounce semisweet chocolate
½ ounce unsweetened chocolate
2 egg whites, at room temperature
Pinch of salt
¼ cup confectioners' sugar
2 egg yolks
1 teaspoon cornstarch
½ teaspoon vanilla extract
Sweetened whipped cream

1.   Set a rack in the bottom of a deep pan large enough to hold a 1-quart bowl. Butter a deep, heat-proof 1-quart bowl. Add water to the pan to a depth of 2 inches. Bring the water to a boil while mixing the pudding.

2.   Melt the butter in a small saucepan. In the top of a double boiler over simmering water, melt the chocolates. Cool both the butter and chocolate, and set aside.

3.   In a small bowl of an electric mixer, beat the egg whites and salt at medium-high speed until they are foamy. Gradually add the confectioners' sugar, beating at high speed until soft peaks form. Set aside.

4.   Put the egg yolks in another small bowl and add, in order, the cornstarch, vanilla, melted butter, and melted chocolate. Whisk until smooth after each addition. Pour this mixture evenly over the egg whites. Fold until blended. Pour the pudding into the prepared buttered bowl and cover with foil.

5.   Set the bowl on the rack in the pan of boiling water. Reduce the heat to medium. Cover the pan and steam the pudding for 30 minutes, or until it is is puffed and a toothpick inserted in center comes out clean. Serve with the whipped cream.

White Grape Tart

This cooling and simple grape tart is refreshingly delicious on a warm summer's afternoon when the tea of choice is iced and the primary pastime is pleasant conversation with dear ones. We suggest making this tart on the day you plan to serve it, as it is quite fragile.

YIELD: 10 servings

Zinfandel sauce:
1/3 *cup all-purpose flour*
1/3 *cup granulated sugar*
Pinch of salt
3 egg yolks
1 cup light cream or milk
1/4 *cup white zinfandel*
2 to 3 drops freshly squeezed lemon juice, optional

Pastry:
1 1/4 *cups all-purpose flour*
3/4 *cup (1 1/2 sticks) butter, chilled and cut into pieces*
1/4 *cup superfine sugar*
Pinch of salt
1 egg, lightly beaten

Filling and Garnish:
3 pounds seedless green grapes (about 7 cups stemmed grapes)
1 egg white
Superfine sugar
Confectioners' sugar
Rose geranium leaves or mint leaves

TO MAKE THE ZINFANDEL SAUCE:

1. Thoroughly mix the flour, sugar, and salt in a heavy 1-quart saucepan. Add the egg yolks and 1/2 cup of the cream and whisk until smooth. Gradually whisk in the remaining cream.

2. Cook the mixture over medium heat stirring constantly with a wooden spoon for about 20 minutes, until the sauce is very thick and glossy. To prevent lumping, it may be necessary to whisk the sauce for the last few minutes of cooking.

3. Pour the sauce into a 1-quart bowl. Lay wax paper directly on its surface and refrigerate for 1 1/2 hours.

4. Take the chilled sauce from the refrigerator and stir in the zinfandel and, if desired, the lemon juice. Cover and chill for at least 4 more hours.

TO MAKE THE PASTRY:

1. In the bowl of a food processor, add the flour, butter, sugar, salt, and egg. Process until the dough forms a ball and pulls away from the sides of the bowl. Shape the dough into a smooth ball and wrap it in plastic. Refrigerate it for 30 minutes.

2. Turn the chilled dough out onto a floured work surface and knead it with the heel of your hand until it is well blended. Using a rolling pin, roll the dough into a 14-inch circle. Drape the dough in an 11-inch tart form with a removable bottom and set on a baking sheet. Press the dough into the tart form and trim the excess. If you prefer, the dough can be patted into the tart form. Cover and refrigerate for 45 minutes.

TO ASSEMBLE THE TART:

1. Preheat the oven to 400°F. Remove the stems from the grapes and wash the grapes briefly in cold water. Dry them well on clean dishtowels or paper towels.

2. Prick the sides and bottom of the chilled tart shell with a fork and bake it for about 25 minutes, or until it is golden brown. If the pastry puffs or bubbles during

baking, prick the bottom of the tart again. Remove the tart from the oven and cool it completely on a wire rack.

3. In a small bowl, beat the egg white with a fork. Place some superfine sugar in a shallow dish or pie plate. Dip 2 cups of grapes first in the egg white and then in the superfine sugar. Dry on wire racks — the grapes will look frosted.

4. Just before serving, combine 3 cups of unfrosted grapes and ⅔ cup of the zinfandel sauce. Spoon the grapes evenly over the bottom of the cooled tart shell. Top with the rest of the unfrosted grapes and sprinkle the tart with confectioners' sugar.

5. Garnish the tart with frosted grapes and fresh rose geranium leaves or mint leaves. Serve the tart with the remaining zinfandel sauce.

A Sweets Tea

Ambrosia Torte

White Grape Tart

Rose Water Sugar Cookies

Feathery Chocolate Pudding

Country French Prune Pudding

Old-Fashioned Sauces for Puddings

Ginger Pear Delight

Rosy Yogurt Cooler

Country French Prune Pudding

For prunes with a bit of an English flavor, soak them for four days in half a cup of port in a lidded pint jar. Shake the jar every so often. When it's time to make the pudding, lift the prunes from the jar with a slotted spoon and follow the recipe, omitting the kirsch.

YIELD: 6 servings.

About 25 (8 ounces) soft, pitted prunes
Finely grated zest of 1 large orange
½ cup plus 1 tablespoon all-purpose flour
Pinch of salt
3 eggs, at room temperature
½ cup granulated sugar
1½ cups milk
4 teaspoons kirsch
Confectioners' sugar
1 cup heavy cream, for serving, optional

1. Preheat the oven to 400°F. Butter a 9½ x 1¼-inch pie plate.

2. Lay the prunes in the pie plate and sprinkle them with the orange zest.

3. In a small bowl of an electric mixer, beat the flour, salt, and 1 egg at medium speed until the flour is moistened. Add the remaining eggs, one at a time, beating well after each addition. Continue beating until the batter is very creamy, about 4 to 5 minutes. With the mixer turned down to medium-low speed, gradually add the granulated sugar, milk, and then the kirsch. Beat until the batter is smooth. Pour the batter over the prunes.

4. Bake for 45 minutes, or until the pudding is puffed and brown.

5. Dust the top of the pudding with confectioners' sugar. Serve with a pitcher of cold heavy cream to pour over the servings.

Blackberry Tarts

Blackberry Tarts

These little tarts are lovely to serve and their sweet cream filling and berries makes them so easy to eat.

YIELD: 6 tarts

Pastry:
1⅓ cups flour
1 tablespoon granulated sugar
¼ teaspoon salt
¼ cup (½ stick) butter
¼ cup lard
2 to 3 tablespoons ice water

Filling and glaze:
1 8-ounce package cream cheese, softened
3 tablespoons confectioners' sugar
½ cup heavy cream
⅛ teaspoon orange extract
¼ cup red currant jelly
2 teaspoons blackberry cordial or crème de cassis
1½ cups fresh blackberries

TO MAKE THE PASTRY:

1.   In a medium bowl, stir together the flour, granulated sugar, and salt. With a pastry blender or 2 knives, cut in the butter and lard until the pieces are pea-size.

2.   Sprinkle 1 tablespoon cold water over the mixture. Toss with a fork, and push the dough to the side of the bowl. Repeat with the remaining water until all the dough is moistened. Shape the dough into a ball, wrap in plastic, and refrigerate for 30 minutes.

3.   Form the chilled dough into 6 equal balls. Between 2 pieces of floured wax paper, press each ball into a 5-inch circle. Press each round into a 4-inch fluted tart pan with a removable bottom and trim off any excess dough. Place the tart pans on a baking sheet and freeze about 15 minutes.

4.   Preheat the oven to 400°F. Prick the cold pastry all over with a fork. Line the pastry shells with small squares of foil and fill the foil with pie weights or dried beans.

5.   Bake for 10 minutes, or until the pastry begins to brown around the edges. Remove the foil and weights. Prick the pastry and bake for 7 to 9 minutes. Cool on a wire rack.

TO MAKE THE FILLING:
In a small bowl of an electric mixer, combine cream cheese and confectioners' sugar at medium speed until blended. With the mixer at low speed, gradually add the heavy cream and orange extract. Beat at medium speed until mixture is thick, about 1 minute.

TO MAKE THE GLAZE:
In small heavy saucepan, melt the jelly and cordial over medium heat, stirring often. Strain the mixture through cheesecloth. Let it cool slightly.

TO ASSEMBLE THE TART:
Spoon the filling into the bottom of each tart shell and arrange blackberries on top of the filling. Spoon the glaze over the berries. Refrigerate the tarts until serving time.

Marmalade Torte Paradiso

Adorned with fresh orange lunettes and flourishes of whipped orange cream, this Marmalade Torte Paradiso is worthy of its name. The torte's orange marmalade and carrots make a sweet marriage of flavors.

YIELD: 8 servings

4 egg yolks
½ cup plus 1 tablespoon sugar
1 scant cup finely ground hazelnuts
1 scant cup finely shredded carrots
2 tablespoons all-purpose flour
2 tablespoons orange marmalade
5 egg whites
Pinch of salt

Marmalade Cream Filling:
1½ cups heavy cream
⅓ cup orange marmalade
Thin orange slices and whipped cream

TO MAKE THE CAKE:

1.   Preheat the oven to 300°F. Butter and flour two 6½ x 3-inch springform pans.
2.   In a medium bowl of an electric mixer, beat the egg yolks and sugar at high speed until they are pale yellow, about 5 minutes. Add the hazelnuts, carrots, flour, and marmalade. Mix well and set aside.

Meanwhile, let us have a cup of tea. The afternoon glow is brightening the bamboos, the fountains are bubbling with delight, the soughing of the pines is heard in our kettle. Let us dream of evanescence, and linger in the beautiful foolishness of things.

Kazuko Okakura
THE BOOK OF TEA

Marmalade Torte Paradiso

3.   In another medium bowl, beat the egg whites and salt at high speed until they are stiff but not dry. Gradually fold the egg whites into the batter. Pour the batter into the prepared pans.
4.   Bake for 45 minutes, until the cakes are browned and just begin to pull away from the sides of the pans. Cool the cakes, still in the pans on wire racks. (The cakes will shrink and fall slightly.)
5.   Loosen the edges of the cakes with a knife, and remove them from the pan. Slice each cake in two layers horizontally. (The layers are very fragile. Use a wide spatula or a flat baking sheet to move them.)

TO MAKE THE MARMALADE CREAM FILLING:
In a small bowl, whip the cream until peaks form. Fold in the marmalade.

TO ASSEMBLE THE TORTE:

1.   Position a cake layer on a serving plate and spread ¼ of the filling on top. Add the other layers of cake with ¼ of the filling spread on each layer, including the top.
2.   Garnish the torte with fresh orange slices. Pipe additional whipped cream atop the torte for decoration. Serve at once.

TEA GLOSSARY

Tea is named in one of two ways: first, according to the region from which it originates such as Darjeeling and Ceylon; and second, because of special blending, such as Earl Grey and Marquis of Queensbury tea. Not all tea comes from the tea plant *camellia sinensis.* Nearly any drink brewed from herbs, spices, flowers, fruits and even bark is called "tea". The most common of these teas are herb teas, also referred to as tisanes. Some flower teas, such as chamomile and elderflower, are also tisanes.

TEAS

Assam: a fine-quality tea from the Assam district of India, where tea was first cultivated by the British and still remains a prized area for strong black teas.

Bancha: the everyday Japanese green tea.

Ceylon: a number of teas bear the name "Ceylon." Now known as Sri Lanka, this country produces some of the best teas in the world.

Darjeeling: a black tea from the part of India of the same name, which is in the foothills of the Himalayas. Darjeeling is considered, by some, the finest tea in the world and is the beverage of choice for many afternoon tea aficionados. Darjeeling is a classic "self drinker," which means it tastes strong and clear on its own, without blending any other tea leaves with it.

Formosa Oolong: a tea from Taiwan, which used to be Formosa, considered to be the best oolong.

Gunpowder: a high-quality green tea from China.

Keemun: an orchid flavored tea that is considered one of the best Chinese black teas.

Lapsang Souchong: a famous black tea from China with a smoky flavor.

Nilgiri: an Indian black tea that is used almost exclusively for blending.

Oolong: a partially fermented tea that is a cross between green and black tea. Oolong tea, which is quite mild, is used for blending with black tea.

Tencha: a Japanese green tea used for tea ceremonies and considered to be the finest green tea available in Japan.

Yunnan: a fragrant and full flavored black tea from a western province of China.

BLENDINGS:

Earl Grey: a favorite blending of black teas the world around. R. Twining and Co. Ltd. originally made this tea for Charles, the second Earl Grey, but in later years other tea companies began marketing a similar blend with the same name. This is the quintessential afternoon tea.

English Breakfast Tea: a popular blending of Indian

and Ceylon teas. Considered brisk enough for early morning, it is also perfectly adequate for afternoon tea.

Jasmine: a very soothing tea, made from jasmine flowers and leaves blended with green tea.

Orange Pekoe: a grade of tea leaf, but also a blending of good quality Ceylon tea leaves. This tea has nothing whatsoever to do with the citrus fruit.

Russian Caravan: a blend of Chinese black tea that was reportedly developed for transporting and drinking on the overland trade route between China and Russia early in the eighteenth century. Some other Chinese teas destined for Russia were first ground into powder and then compressed into bricks for easy packing. The bricks were shaved as needed for brewing with boiling water.

FRUIT TEAS AND TISANES:

Apple; Peach; Strawberry; Mango: four popular fruit teas made from the leaves and parts of the fruit.

Lemon Verbena: a tea tasting faintly of lemon and reported to reduce fever and arthritis pain.

Lemon; Orange: citrus fruits — the skins and leaves — that yield popular, refreshing teas.

Orange Blossom; Lotus; Rose; Chrysanthemum; Chamomile: a few different flower teas made from the petals and often the leaves of these flowers. All are gentle and fragrant.

Peppermint: made from crushed peppermint, or other mint leaves. This is a soothing tonic, especially for an upset stomach.

Rosehip: a bright red tea made from dried rosehips. This is a very good overall tonic for mild day-to-day ailments.

Thyme: a tea made from the dried leaves, flowers and stems of cultivated garden thyme plants.

TEA EQUIPMENT

The Victorians, many of whom acquired great wealth during the nineteenth century, collected, among many other things, all sorts of fancy and elaborate tea implements. Silversmiths and other artisans created instruments specially designed for tasks that could just as easily been accomplished in other, if more mundane, ways.

Today, we require far fewer implements at teatime, and indeed, many of us may never own a silver tea service. Still, there exists healthy curiosity, and sometimes mild amusement about this popular teatime impedimenta.

Caddy Spoon: These spoons were used to measure tea from the caddy. Silversmiths often fashioned them to resemble shells, as the Chinese frequently used real shells to scoop loose tea.

Mote Spoon: Used to skim stray tea leaves mote spoons are made from perforated silver and sometimes have a sharp point, which is used to clean the spout of the pot.

Muffin Dish: Since hot muffins, just toasted in the kitchen, were popular for tea, silver muffin dishes were designed with domed lids and hot water reservoirs beneath the dish to keep the muffins toasty warm.

Sugar Sifter; Muffineer: Shaped like a large salt or pepper shaker, these are filled with sugar or a combination of sugar and cinnamon for sprinkling on hot buttered muffins.

Sugar Tongs: Sugar tongs were more popular when sugar was served in cubes. They are most often made from silver, and may be tweezer-shaped or scissor-handled.

Tea Caddy: Caddies are containers designed to hold loose tea leaves. They were artfully fashioned from wood, porcelain, silver or glass. Most Victorian households had at least two caddies, one for black tea, the other for green. Caddies were often kept under lock and key, to dissuade the servants from sampling the tea.

Tea Cozy: Although tea cozies were never seen at grand Victorian tea parties, they have been common in most British households since the nineteenth century. They are typically made from quilted fabric and slip over a teapot to help keep the tea warm.

Tea Strainer: These pretty strainers are designed to fit over the teacup and to catch leaves that escape from the pot when the tea is poured.

Tea Tray: Oval-shaped tea trays are made from silver or Sheffield-plate. They have a trim and a functional handle on each end for carrying. Tea trays are large enough to hold the tea service and teacups.

Tea Urn: This is a large decorative vessel for brewed tea. It is fitted with a spigot to facilitate filling smaller teapots.

Teacups: Teacups were originally shaped like coffee cups, which are less rounded. Today, a proper teacup is made from fine bone china and is slightly round with a wide, generous mouth. Early European tea and coffee cups had no handles but as afternoon tea became fashionable, handles were added to prevent ladies from burning their fingers.

Teakettle: Today, teakettles sit on stoves and are used to boil water for tea and other cooking tasks. In Victorian times, the teakettle was filled with boiling water in the kitchen and then transported to the drawing room. The kettle was set on a trivet above a spirit lamp to keep the water hot. Often, it was hinged to the trivet so that the kettle had only to be tipped for easy pouring.

Teapot: The finer teapots were made from sterling, although today many purists feel tea does not taste as good when served from a silver pot as it does from porcelain. The earliest teapots were designed similarly to straight sided coffee and chocolate pots, but over the years they became more rounded.

Teapoy: A teapoy, a term introduced by the English who had lived in India, is a three-legged table designed to hold tea caddies and mixing containers.

INDEX

PERMISSIONS
AND PHOTOGRAPHY CREDITS

62: Photograph by John Kane.

63: Photograph by Jim Hedrich.

64: Photograph by Kathlene Persoff.

65: Photograph by Joshua Greene.

68: Photograph by William P. Steele.

72: Photograph by Jeff McNamara.

74: Photograph by Jim Hedrich.

76: Photograph by Jim Hedrich.

78: Photograph by William P. Steele.

83: Photograph by Joshua Greene.

84: Photograph by John Kane.

88: Photograph by William P. Steele.

89: Photograph by Joshua Greene.

92-93: Photograph by Starr Ockenga.

RECIPE CREDITS

Philis Bennett: *Mint Tea, Milk and Honey Bread with Honey Butter, Currant Scones with Smoked Turkey, Ginger-Flavored Honey, Herb-Flavored Honey, Berry-Flavored Honey, Rose Water Sugar Cookies, Honey Tart, Marmalade Torte Paradiso*

Michelle Berriedale-Johnson: *Stilton, Pear, and Watercress Savory*

Carole Clark and John Manikowski: *Country Peach and Plum Tart*

Suzanne Corbett: *Herbed Cream Cheese Sandwiches, Black Walnut Linzer Hearts*

Kevin Crafts: *Lemon-Mint Tea, Orange-Spice Tea, Strawberry Tea, Iced Clove Cooler, Cucumber Sandwiches with Mint Butter, Lemon Bread, Blackberry Muffin Miniatures, Lime Wafers, Madeleines*

John Durkin and Diane Margaritis: *Lemon Ginger Pound Cake, Chocolate Walnut Torte*

Ronald Gibson: *Currant and Pecan Scones, Gingerbread Girls and Boys, Hickory Nut Butter Cakes*

Yanny Hartman: *Pumpkin Nut Bread, Pumpkin Biscuits*

John Hudspeth and Marion Cunningham: *Heavenly Hots, Raised Waffles*

Donna Tabbert Long: *Blackberry Syrup, Spiced Blackberry Jam, Blackberry Jam Cake, Blackberry Tarts*

Susan Mason: *Salmon Mousse, Sage Bread*

Joy McConnell: *Spinach Cheese Tartlets*

Jeanne Nakjavani and Linda Underhill: *White Winter Champagne Punch*

Lynn Ringland: *Jam Cookies, Dream Cookies, Meringue Kisses, Ambrosia Torte*

Renee Shepherd: *Lemon Thyme Bread, Compound Herb Butter*

Sylvia Thompson: *Old-Fashioned Sauces for Puddings, Feathery Chocolate Pudding, Country French Prune Pudding*

Emelie Tolley: *Orange-Clove Tea, Lovers' Tea, Vanilla Milk Tea, Lavender and Lime, Ginger Pear Delight, Rosy Yogurt Cooler, Double Lemon Punch, Watercress Sandwiches, Cinnamon Raisin Roll-Ups, Orange Honey, Sage Cheese Butter, Tarragon-Mustard Butter, Strawberry Butter, Grilled Marmalade Fingers, Raspberry and Lemon Curd Hearts, Lily of the Valley Cake, White Grape Tart*